DAY T... FOR BEGINNERS 2020

A Guide with Everything You Need to Make Money from Today. You Will Learn to Trade With Simple and Proven Strategies to Profit from The Stock Market.

ROBERT SMILE

Table Of Contents:

Introduction

A large portion of day trading individuals is the employees of banks and other financial institutions. This group of employees tasked with such roles is always competent specialists in managing funds and equity investment. The year 1975 saw the popularization of day trading with several parties joining the trade. It was because the commissions in the United States were deregulated. The rise of electronic platforms for trading was witnessed in the years of 1990s. The volatility of stock prices was also seen during the periods of the dot-com bubble, as represented in figure 1 below. Scalping is a new intraday trading technique that is used by traders in the day trading. It involves holding the trading position for a couple of minutes or seconds.

Process of Day Trading

The process of day trading involves sloppy financial leverage, and speedy returns are probable. This phenomenon makes the trade to either be extremely profitable or extremely unprofitable. Those people who are described as high-risk profile traders are also significantly impacted by such an event. These groups of traders have the probability of making enormous percentages of profit or, on the other hand, undergo massive amounts of percentage loss. Day trading trader's individuals are sometimes referred to as bandits or gamblers by other traders or investors. It is because these traders can either make vast amounts of profits or losses during the trade.

Several factors can make this form of trade to be very risky while an individual is trading. They include individual trading on a deal with low odds instead of trading on one that has high odds of winning; the presence of risk capital that is inadequate, which is tied together with overload stress of surviving and presence of poor management of funds which entails poor execution of the trade.

Gains and losses are mostly amplified by the widespread usage of buying on margin. The process of buying on margin can be described as the use of borrowed funds. This action usually results in a trader experiencing a substantial loss or gain in a short span during the day. Brokers have the common tendency of allowing more significant trade margins for day traders.

Short Trades and Long Trades

The terms regarding short trades are common terms to an individual who is participating in stock trading. These terms are majorly used in situations where a trader is either buying or selling first. There are several expectations that a trader always has in mind if he or she is either doing short trade or long trade. When a trader is participating in a short trade, he or she purchases the financial instruments intending to sell them at a higher price in the future to make profits. On the other hand, short trade involves a trader selling financial instruments with the intent of later buying them at a lower price to make his or her profits.

Long Trade

Various day traders are participants that are common in the long trade. They purchase financial instruments with hopes that they will increase in value. This makes their prices rise in turn. The term that is mostly used by day traders is always buy and long, which are interchangeable. Software developed to help long trade, with buttons that are either marked long or buy. These buttons are used to represent an open position entered by a trader. This position simply means an individual has shares in a certain firm or trade.

If a trader decides to go long, he or she is always interested in purchasing a specific financial instrument. If the decision for such is perused, the potential for profit levels is always unlimited. It is because the prices of the purchased financial instruments can get higher indefinitely. This is despite a day trader participating in small moves. The risks in this form of trade have lower risk potential of the purchased instruments to fall to zero. It is because profits and risks are always controlled by the multiple small moves that are made.

Short Trade

Day traders in short trades always sell their financial instruments before purchasing them. During moments they buy the financial instrument, they hope the prices will have gone. This the moment they can realize their profits because they will be buying the financial instruments at a lower price from that which they had sold. Short trading is one of the most confusing forms of trade because people across the globe are used to buying first before selling. However, one can be able to sell and buy in the financial markets.

There are common terms that are used by traders participating in short trades. These terms include short and sell, which are used interchangeably. Software developed to aid short trade also has buttons marked short or sell. The term short usually means a trader has an open position to shorting some financial instruments. Profit levels are always limited in this situation when compared to the initial amount that was used to purchase the financial instruments. Various traders are used to taking short positions to reduce or minimize risks.

How to Manage Risks in Day Trading

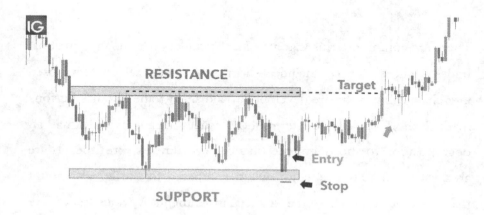

The first thing you need to know as a trader is that you will run volumes of trades and experience a lot of risks. Trading the markets is one of the riskiest investment techniques, and many people go for day trading because they have the potential for higher gains over a short period. If you have a small account, day trading gives you the chance to grow small accounts in such a short timeframe.

Risk comes about because you have to execute hundreds of trades in such a short time. You also have the capacity to place any trade you want, for as low as $500 or as high as $25,000 in a single trade. The trades are also at high speed, which means the market can swing any way—up or down. The direction of the market determines whether you make a loss or a profit.

Day trading gives you two realms of strategies to go with—high-risk trading strategies or low-risk strategies. The goal of a successful trader is to maximize profit while lowering risks. Every time you place a trade, you need to evaluate the risk of the trade and then weigh it against the potential reward. Often times, this is made worse by our emotional reaction to various price directions. For instance, since you experienced a loss recently, the next logical step would be to take a higher risk on the next trade so that you can compensate for the loss. Experienced traders have a heightened level of awareness that they use to recognize a loss and reward and will make sure they take the right decision. However, you have to learn the skill over time.

You can develop a sense of decision making by keeping a journal as you trade and then reviewing the notes after the close of the market.

Different Types of Risk

When talking about risk, you need to consider the different types in order for you to understand what we are saying. As a day trader, your primary role is to know the distance between the entry and the stop. Stop loss needs to be based on a resistance area on the chart or recent support.

The majority of your losses need to happen when a trade hits the stop price. This means you won't make any profit on whatever you are trading.

The second type of risk is the volatility of the market. As day traders, volatility is a friend to all of us, but it is also risky because markets that are extremely volatile tend to result in higher losses than what you actually planned for. Since there is a sense of inherent risk in trading, you need to try and avoid placing a trade when the volatility cannot be predicted, for instance, when there is breaking news.

The other type of risk is exposure risk. Exposure results when you multiply the price of shares by the number of held shares. As an investor, you increase this risk when you hold on positions for a very long time. To mitigate this risk, you need to hold onto shares for a short time.

If you are holding onto large positions for a long time, you stand to experience stock halts. Halts can take hours or days, though they are rare. The most common halts are those waiting for the release of news or volatility halts. Anytime a stock halts, it can lead to a different price. The biggest risk is that the stock might reopen at a very different price, which might be lower than the current price of the stock. You can take steps to reduce the effect of the halts by understanding what leads to the halts in the first place.

Journaling

If you are looking at a routine that is easy to implement and can change the way you trade, then think about keeping a journal. The journal is a little black book that details what you do each day.

The aim of keeping a journal is to help improve your setups so that you use your experiences to analyze and help refine your trading while you improve the whole experience.

Here, we look at all you need to come up with a journal and maintain it.

What Is a Journal?

A trading journal is a way to keep track of what you are doing on daily basis as a day trader. You jot down notes of what you do each day, especially the different trades (or lack of) and the results of any action you take.

The trading journal needs to be tailored to your trading styles and preferences. You can keep the journal in a physical notebook or a detailed digital document on your computer. Regardless of the format, when maintained with due diligence, the trading journal can be the best way to make you a better day trader.

How Does the Trading Journal Help You Achieve Better Trades?

There are a number of ways in which a trading journal will help you become better at what you do.

Many traders attribute their success in creating and maintaining a trading journal. By noting down the different trades, you are able to check the progress over time. This allows you to find out what is working or not and change or modify them to succeed.

Helps You Develop Discipline in Trading

Having a trading journal helps you develop discipline as you trade. How does it do so? Well, it forces you to follow the guidelines that you have set down.

The sense of accountability that you get when you have a trading journal makes sure you are responsible for research and trading. If you know what you need to keep a log each day, you do it without fail. Making sure you log your trades and whatever happens, requires a lot of discipline. Good habits such as these require you to go straight when executing trades.

Helps You Master Your Emotions

One of the top suggestions to help you run trades the right way is to trade like you are not human. Machines do not have emotions and approach all the processes in a scientific way.

However, this is easier said than done. When you get in a position to lose money, usually, you find it tough getting emotion out of the way.

Having a journal can help you keep the emotions out of the way. With a journal in place, you get to keep track of how you feel emotionally in various trading stages. This is just to keep the emotions in check.

With time, you realize that there is a pattern that is emerging, for instance, you might find yourself getting calmer and taking orders the right way each time.

Improves Your Risk Management Practices

Day trading comes with a high level of risk. This is something that you cannot change at all because it is the nature of the market for things to run this way. However, there are various ways in which you can mitigate these risks. For one, you need to invest a large amount of research and study to give you the knowledge that you need to choose the least risky trades possible.

With a journal, you can learn things about risk tolerance. For instance, you might find that you have consistently been able to hold positions for longer and you have been losing profits as a result. You might also find that you have issues getting out of trades because you have been taking positions that are too big for your stage.

By looking at the risks that you have been taking and how they affect the results you return, you get to make adjustments.

For instance, you might exit trades sooner or you might end up taking smaller positions based on the results you return. This way, you help reduce risks and improve risk management.

Know How to Set Stops and Profit

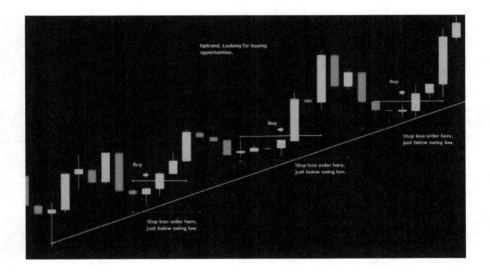

The Entry

Many people out there feel that the entry is the least important part of day trading that there is. And some people think that a random entry is good enough to gain a profit from. Although many people feel that way, you should always carefully consider it as a part of your day trading system. There are actually two important reasons why you need to consider the entry. The first reason is volatility and the second reason is risk.

The trading setup can be configured so that volatility is relatively low for two reasons:

- Expansion: You want to enter the trade right before a period of expansion since high volatility usually follows on the heels of low volatility. The expansion is what takes us right into the profit zone!

- Risk: It usually feels like we can't control a thing during stock day trading. But the low volatility gives us the opportunity to control at least one thing. Yep! We can control how much we are going to risk on the trade! Since the point is to keep our risk at an absolute bare minimum, we use the areas with small range bars to put our stops under. If you aren't paying attention to your entry setups, the initial stop will be too far away from your entry and the risk you take on will be too high!

The Stop

Yes. Here it is again. You will hear a lot about the stop, and here we will go into it in even more detail. I want to explain it a little further and once again reiterate its importance. It is definitely the one-day trading rule that you can safely bet all of your money on. And it should always be the first concept that comes to your mind as you are experimenting and coming up with new systems or methods.

At some point, as you begin talking to other day traders, you will hear someone say that they don't use stops period. Unless they are using some magic trading system that will put them back into a trade in a winning direction, then it's a crazy idea. Using the stop is your money's earliest line of defense. Since you are reading this and you are probably new to day trading, I will remind you again. Always, always, decide where you are going to place your stops before you remotely decide to enter the trade!

What the Stop Does for You

Winning trades are fantastic and they tell you that what you are doing is right and is working. However, most likely, the odds are that you will be using a day trading system that will bring you more losing trades than winning trades. But don't get upset! We all start somewhere! And how do we learn without mistakes? Right? At this moment, you need to understand why you need to use stops and why they are so important because you are going to get stopped out of a ton of trades. And that's perfectly ok. It's normal to have many losing trades.

This is what's going to take place if you don't use a system with stops. You are going to end up calling your broker to ask him to send you a check for the small remaining balance on your account. Then you will go back to your desk, scratch your head, and try to come up with a trading system using those stops. So, it would be wise to just include them the first time.

When you begin trading, you will decide for yourself what the amount of loss you are willing to accept per trade. It might be decided based on volatility, percentage movement, etc. No matter what method you use to determine your limit, the stop will act as your line in the sand. There is one big no for you to be aware of. Do not get into the practice of moving your stops out and away from the price as the time for it to stop you outgrows closer. You will be screwed. It may not appear that way at first; you might see that it will help you on a few trades. However, in the end, you will be screwed, so just don't get into the habit of doing it. Having wider stops may, of course, mean that you have a higher percentage of winning trades, but it also means that when you have a losing trade that it will be higher.

The Exit

Just as important as considering your stops, you should consider your exits. You want your day trading systems to have a positive expectancy. You need to make enough profit out of your trades or you will run the risk of a negative expectancy. We will cover expectancy in more depth later, but you need to know this information about it right now. If you have a negative expectancy, you will basically be wasting both your time and your money!

You can never control whether your trade will be a winner or loser. However, just like a stop that you use to control what your loss will be, you use the exit to control what your profit will be. The exit strategy that you use has to allow your trade some wiggle room, but not get you out too soon.

The Exit Objective

You want to see your average profitable trade be higher than your average non-profitable trade. You should set your profit objectives for more than the stop amount you have on your trade. In order to make a consistent profit, your day trading system has to allow the winning trades to take off and run, so that you are averaging sufficiently more than you are averaging on your losing trades.

Profit Targets

This is a nice, simple, and effective exit method that can be placed inside of your trading platform. It is placed at a dollar amount away from the entry price that you decided to enter. The great thing is that once you put this in place, you have nothing to do. You can completely leave your computer. You can go eat, or clean, or do whatever you need to do. Because no matter what, you can't control what happens with the prices after you set your profit target. And by walking away from the computer, it will keep you from messing around with your trade as you have set it up. It would be natural for you to mess around with your trade if you just sat there at the computer, watching the prices go up or down. If you just walk away and let it go, what's the worst that can happen? The price will hit your stop, hit your profit target, or be somewhere in the middle.

Position Sizing

Position sizing is really very simple; however, it is the least understood trading concept.

The whole idea behind position sizing is to prepare you for losing streaks and to get you through them. Regardless of how great your method is, you will have them. It's also referred to as trading money management. Position sizing has nothing to do with initial stops or exits. That's the focus on the number of stocks or futures or whatever that you will trade.

Let's take a look at two different position sizing methods. The first one is the easiest. It's so easy, in fact, a child can understand it. The second method is still fairly easy, but more detailed and actually, it's the better way to manage your risk.

Learn to Trade Avoiding Beginner Mistakes

Playing out of your depth: Scared money never wins.

Fear freezing thinking: Analysis paralysis.

While doing your practice trading, pay close attention to how much your trades vary in profit/loss during each 5-minute segment, how much it varies in 15 minutes, half-hour, hour, and so on. Don't do this just one day or one hour but over several days or even a couple of weeks. The reason to do this is quite simple: You are, so-to-speak, "testing your risk tolerance." Admittedly, there is a difference between paper trading and using real money. Still, it is better that you get this experience than not. If you feel these variations are not acceptable for any reason, this type of trading may not be for you.

It is normal for you to have some 'analysis paralysis,' especially the moment as you switch to trading real money instead of practice trading. If your brain is overwhelmed so completely with all you are trying to learn, be patient with yourself. Give yourself enough time for your brain to assimilate the process. With practice, your thinking and reactions become faster. You will also notice the points at which you start stressing during losing trades; take some notes on this because you need to know how this amount to determine your risk tolerance and experience the point where your decisions are triggered by emotions. By the time you can practice trade and accomplish 25 consecutive "successful" (error-free, whether winner or loser) trades, you will be able to get some idea of what risk level you can handle.

Using a Blind System and Using Technical Blindly

By "blind system," I mean those get-rich-quick scams that promise lots of money with very little work, risk, or thought. Buyers beware. No one who would ever sell you such a system will ever agree to pay your losses. Trading blind on promises from unproven sources—is risky territory.

Remember that technical indicators are tools, not foolproof trading systems, and must be used in the context of market concepts, trends, and patterns.

Impatience and Not Preparing Well Enough

Think of trading as owning your own business. You invest a few bucks for information and supplies, then a research period to test feasibility as best as you can, and then risk your hard-earned money. I strongly suggested you practice trade with a ledger, keeping notes until you can string together 25 consecutive trades with no errors. It takes time to do this successfully. Be patient and take time to learn by doing, not just reading about it. Remember, no two traders are identical; find what works for you.

Ignore Brain Pattern Dominance

When you trade using technical charting and indicators, you will notice that you start to "see" a lot of potential patterns that can be forming. This is apophenia; your brain working hard to find patterns and project outcomes. This is normal. Wait and let the "market tell you" what is going on, and don't allow your attention to stray when your brain sends you all the possible outcomes of things that are not yet in your charts and indicators. Until you gain some experience, this is one of the most difficult things to learn. Trading with technical indicators and charts is not a perfect science by any means. The indicators will sometimes lead you astray no matter how long you study them. It is quite common for inexperienced traders to think that if only they find the right technical indicators, they will win the vast majority of trades. This is a very popular myth. It is somewhat almost everyone wants to believe.

It is a beginner's mistake to think that just because you got a good night's sleep, got up early, read the day's financial news or financial channel, and have spent hours of practice—the market will send you a perfect technical indicator trade in the first ten minutes of your trading. You must have patience. Sometimes, you see a trade instantly. Other times you can go more than an hour and see no chances at all. Other days, you'll have almost too many good signals. These things do not happen on a schedule. You will see some days that are volatile and fast, maybe too fast for your risk tolerance. Other days will be so slow, you might feel bored and that you've wasted time. Over time, you learn to recognize those time periods—when trying to trade at all is impossible, so don't. Some days as the saying goes, "You get all dressed up and there is just no place to go." Hope is not a strategy. Let the market tell you what's happening, not the other way around.

Over-Using Genius of Hindsight

This is another of the "most common" mistakes new and veteran traders make. I've already written extensively about this. You can learn from genius of hindsight, but you should never judge your ability to trade with information you did not have during the trade. This may seem counter-intuitive, so I want to be perfectly clear about this: You can learn from hindsight; it can be a debriefing. Recognize that judging your decisions with hindsight is always a hypothetical matter, never based on the same facts you had before or during a trade.

Trying to Guess Reversals

There are times when you may have a strong bias about what the market "should" do. For example, The market may have extended time periods of remarkable gains or losses. You come to feel the market should be ready for some reaction, retracement, or some adjustment. Times like this will give you a strong bias and it is too easy to forget that you could be considering trading on that bias, even though the technical indicators or other market action is telling you otherwise.

Over time, you will learn to use your technical charts and indicators, much like a night aircraft pilot uses instruments to navigate. It is quite common to 'over-read' your indicators like the MACD. By that, I mean you will naturally start to anticipate what might happen next and trade on this speculation, rather than waiting for a more reliable signal. To allow yourself to follow this inclination is to run the extra risk of ignoring your charting and indicators. Avoiding this mistake takes an enormous amount of patience and a bit of experience.

Letting Recent Experience Skew Your Thinking

So, what does "your recent experience" really mean? To a stock trader, it could mean last year or last month. To a day-trader, it could mean 15 minutes ago, yesterday, or two hours ago or even five minutes ago. When a day trader has a string of consecutive losses, it can result in the trader being less aggressive and overly cautious. This can materialize into a reaction of: a) taking profits too quickly to "make up" for the losing trades, b) perhaps letting the losses accumulate due to being hopeful, or c) exiting a trade in a small drawdown too quickly to avoid more losses. Any of these three reactions as a result of recent losing trades can be directly categorized as letting your emotions influence your trading decisions.

The answer to this problem is to learn to rely on the experience you gain using the candlesticks and MACD. Over time, you will gain more confidence in your ability to read market news, to be aware of scheduled reports and major events that occur during a trading day and will better understand how to interpret the various intensities of trading signals. As you gain experience with reading candlesticks and using the MACD indicator—you will learn to rely more on these things—than to listen to that voice in your head that brings emotional reactions as well as its ability to find patterns that are really not there, those optical illusions due to apophenia and pareidolia. Each trade you make is no more related to the last trade than is one-coin toss that follows another. They are mutually exclusive, even though your brain is hard-wired to relate them. This first step in avoiding this is to be aware of it.

Not Evaluating Your Trading as a Business Plan

You must keep a clear and accurate trading log. You'll be using it to evaluate your methods and results. It will be the equivalent of a business ledger that records expenses (losses) and profits and it will detail your methods. It is easily possible to over-think everything. The ledger you keep will show you truthful results and it can be used to identify both mistakes and to help find improvements you can make. Eventually, you will be your own business manager and can inspect your books to see how your business is doing. Your account balance won't lie, it will tell you if you are doing things right.

There Is No Such Thing as a Winning Streak

There is a sure amount of euphoria when you make money trading. There is always a temptation to think you are on a roll, but this is only an illusion. Each of your trades must justify its own risk-reward.

How to Generate Passive Income

Before you start trading, look around the market and make your plan on which combination of currencies will you trade. Planning also includes the time that you are willing to sit down and monitor the trades, make sure that you stick to the time scheduled to avoid messing up the already earned profit. Remember that choosing the time to trade should be at a time when the market is more active. The market will be there tomorrow and, therefore, when your scheduled time closes your trades. The strategy to be used throughout the time you are trading should also be thought out before you start trading, and it should be adhered to throughout the trading period in the day.

When day trading, you have to know how to manage your money because at the end of the day you want to have money, not lose money. During the day, you will take part in several trades, and therefore you need to know the amount of money you will use to invest. You have to prepare for losses and gains, but the total loss you expect is of importance to avoid losing all your money at the end of the day. This starts by knowing the risk per trade; this is the amount of money you are ready to lose on one trade. If you are a rookie, it is good to set your risk at a maximum of 2%. The size of the account should also be taken into account. If you have a trade that, according to you, has a stop-loss of close to 50 pips, if you risk $200, your risk will be $4. This is done by dividing the amount of money you are risking by the stop loss pips.

Always have a stop target before you start trading, and also consider the type of market you are trading in; there are markets that are so dynamic such that your stop order might not be executed as per the set value. Therefore, to be safe, set your stops using the actual price-action and the conditions prevailing in the market, it is good to set them around the resistance, support levels, chart patterns, trend lines, and how volatile the currencies you are using are in the market. It is not only the stop loss position that you should consider during day trading, but also consider the point at which you want to take profits. For maximum profit, place appropriate levels of taking profit.

In addition, you should look at the reward-risk ratio, and when it is 1:1, it means that the amount you are risking equal to what you expect as a profit, and 3:1 has a triple amount to gain to lose. You can mix these such trades such that you have many with a high potential of gaining and few with an equal potential of winning. You can do it the other way around, but make sure that there is a balance that will leave you with some profit.

Although trading takes place at all times in the world, each market region has its own hours of trade. Therefore, as a trader, you should know your market and its opening and closing hours. You should also know that trading is not good throughout a trading day, and trading is good when the market activity is high. We have four major trading markets, and each of them has its own opening and closing hours. However, there are markets that open around the same time. For example, Tokyo market open at 7 P.M and close at 4 A.M while the Sydney market opens at 5 P.M until 2 A.M looking at the opening hours of the two markets, there is a time when they are all open, therefore, the level of activity with the currencies increases in the two markets between 5 P.M and 8 P.M when you are in the two markets, it is the best time to trade. This means that when more than one market is open at the same time, the trading activities are heightened, and the price of currencies fluctuates more. Therefore, maximize this by doing trades during the time when the market is very active.

You should also be alert on any news release that can make the price of the currency to fluctuate as you look out for changes in prices. Remember that the news can go against the predicted trend, and if you had already taken a position, you can either lose or gain, and it happens in seconds. You can make money by reacting correctly and within the correct time in day trading. The news to look out for is the GDP data, trade deficits, central bank meetings and announcements, consumer confidence, among other big news affecting the economy in the region.

As you look out for the fluctuations in prices, stay in check not to open so many trades that you cannot control. Having many trades does not mean that you will get a lot of money. The best thing to do is to start your trade in small portions. Identify three trades that show potential and monitor the trends; it is good to deal with two trades in a day that you will maximize on their profits than dealing with many that you will not make money on.

The amount of money made in the day also depends on the type of trading strategy used. To make more money choose a trading system that will give you more. When using scalping, it can help you to gain more, but you should increase the number of trades because the income obtained from one trade is very small. This is done when your main strategy is scalping. You can do more than one hundred trades in a day so that at the end of the day you have many wins than losses thus at the end of the day you have good money in your wallet.

If you are doing scalping as a supplementary strategy, you should use it when the market is not giving a large range in terms of the fluctuation of prices of currencies. Then, often, there are no trends in a longer time frame, and therefore using scalping in the short time frame becomes the best option to exploit. This way, you are assured that even without visible trends, there is a possibility that you will not end the day without money. This means that you initiate a long-time frame trade, and as it develops, you start new sets of trade with a shorter time frame; it should be done in the same direction. You will then be entering and leaving the trade, as you collect small amounts, then later get a major profit with the long-time frame.

In a day, you can also use the false breakouts to make money in day trading. Looking at a trend, you can spot a breakout that you believe that it will not maintain the same direction. This is when you make a move, when the trend comes back to its original line; using this quick realization, you can make some cash. Using a fading breakout is the most effective because breakout tends to come out and out, and eventually, they succeed, with a fading breakout, you will be sure of making money. The rationale of using breakouts is that the resistance and support levels are known as ceilings and price floors respectively, and when one of them is broken, traders expect the trend to continue in that direction and therefore, the traders react in the opposite direction, which later stabilizes the trend to its original flow. An example is that when the resistance level is broken, most traders think that the price will continue in the upward trend and buy the currency instead of selling. You should, therefore, sell the currency, acting contrary to what everyone is doing, and when the breakout returns to normal, you buy again at a lower price. Similarly, when the support is broken, it means that the movement of the price is downwards, and most traders are likely to sell and not buy. To collect funds from this move, you should buy the currency instead of selling, and when the price resumes to its trend line, you sell it out. This type of trading is much profitable, but it can be very risky, therefore, analyze the graph well to make sure that it is a false breakdown before you enter the trade. However, to be safer, place a limit order when buying and selling, and make sure that at the end of the day, you have money in your wallet.

You can also make money using pivot points, which helps you to determine how prices of currencies are moving. Most of the time, the pivot points will identify prices as bullish or bearish, then represent the averages for the low, high prices, and closing prices occurring on a trading day. Do you need to know the market trend? The pivot points will help you with that. Use the pivot points to determine the general direction of the trade; if the market price of the currency is above the base of the pivot point, it suggests that the trade is bullish, and when it is below the pivot base, then it is bearish. In addition, when using pivot points, close all the long position trades when the market gets to the resistance levels and close the short ones when the market goes below the support level.

There is also the use of a reversal strategy that is commonly used around the globe; this strategy will help you to make money within a very short time, especially if the currency is moderately volatile. To use this strategy, you will have to study the graph to determine whether it has several consecutive highs and lows. At the highest point, which is called the top, you can easily predict that the price of the currency will reverse, and then react immediately by selling the currency. Similarly, if the graph of the currency has the lowest point, which is known as the bottoms, you predict that the trend will reverse, and buy the currency. When using this strategy, as long as you have predicted the reversal of the trend correctly, you will add money to your wallet.

The red and green indicators can also be used to make money, especially at the beginning of a trading day. The red indicators show that the closing price for the currency was more than the opening price, and the green indicator shows that the closing price was lower than the opening price. The green indicator shows that the price of the currency is likely to increase, especially during the first hours of the opening of the market. This is because the traders will anticipate an upward trend, and start selling, however, you should exchange the currency, and then have a closer observation that will help you exchange again quickly when there is a reverse in the trend.

Manage Emotions

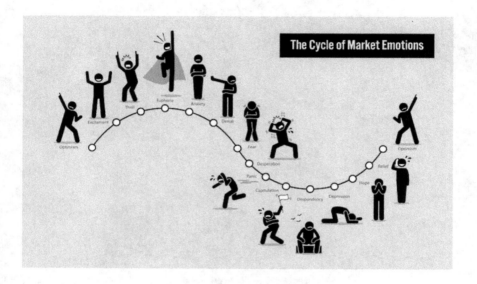

Emotions are at the center of the human experience. Our first line knee jerk reactions to experiences, people, and phenomena are always on an emotional level. We can, therefore, not ignore the impact that emotions have on our ability to successfully navigate through life in terms of relationships, career, and business.

Emotional intelligence is now widely recognized as an instrumental factor for success both in the workplace and personal levels. The ability to not only recognize but also manage your emotions will go a long way in ensuring that the decisions you make are based on logic and not on emotional highs and lows. A key tenement of emotional intelligence is self-awareness. Self-awareness requires you to be aware of what you are feeling and also identify the trigger or triggers that make you feel a particular aware. To be self-aware, you will need to practice self-analysis through reflection to identify the behavioral tendencies that you develop based on your emotional weather. While it may sound like a straightforward concept, emotional reactions occur on a subconscious level and you would be surprised at how many times we make emotion-driven decisions without even being aware of it.

Detaching Emotion From the Stock

Emotions and trading simply don't mix. In addition to greed and fear, traders must be willing not to get attached to their stocks. Stock investments will constantly change. There will be times where it is the wisest move to invest in one stock and not another. However, traders will often become quite attached to a particular stock. The investor must be able to let go of stocks that simply aren't beneficial for them to hold on to. There is no guarantee for how well a stock will perform, as the market is constantly changing, and stocks will change, too. Investors must separate themselves from their stocks and learn when to let a particular stock go.

When trading, it is important to separate logic from emotion. Trading is a numbers game. It's all about what will benefit the trader in the long-term. While it may be easy to let fear or greed take over, to let one's mistakes hinder their future performance, or to become attached to a particular stock, these are not beneficial for one's performance. The trader must adopt a certain mindset and familiarize themselves with the proper psychology of trading. Doing so will definitely be highly beneficial to the trader.

What is Stoicism?

Stoicism can be defined as a school of ancient Greek Romano philosophy. It was founded by a philosopher and thinker named Zeno of Citium. Stoicism is one of four major schools of philosophy that were prevalent in ancient Greece. The other three are Epicurus' Garden, Aristotle's Lyceum, and Plato's Academy.

The Stoic philosophy teaches us how to live a fulfilling life without all the unnecessary stress, depression, anxiety, worry, and all other negative issues. The teachings focus on four main ideas in their teachings. These are control, nature, emotions, and value.

According to the Stoics, there are only very few things that we have control over. These include decisions that we make and the actions that we take. Most things that occur to us are often beyond our control. As such, we tend to be unhappy, stressed out, angry, and so on due to factors that are beyond our control. This is the major mistake that most people make and hence the source of their unhappiness. We need to focus on the few things that we have control over. Only then we will be able to find happiness and tranquility.

When it comes to emotions, we often encounter two main types, mostly. These are emotions of happiness and also those of anger and dejection. Many times, we tend to make mistakes and suffer the consequences. Life is difficult and challenging, and most people accept that. Instead of letting these issues bother us, we should focus on the things that we can change. When we harbor harmful thoughts and emotions based on flawed thinking and emotions, then we really solve nothing at all.

According to stoicism principles, we humans thrive when we accept the things that occur to us. As humans, we should not allow ourselves to be disillusioned by our fear of suffering and pain or controlled by our desires for wealth and pleasure. This is possible through understanding that our powers are limited. We are only able to control a number of things in our lives. The rest of the things that occur to us are beyond our control.

It is advisable, therefore, to understand the way the world works and to play our part as far as nature is concerned. It is crucial that we focus on understanding the way that the world works and to play each one a part in nature. Stoicism also supports just and fair treatment of every person and working together in harmony.

Develop a Morning Routine

You need to have a defined morning routine. The first step as soon as you wake up is to prepare yourself mentally for the tasks ahead. The world is a tough place. We can expect to meet horrible and unreasonable people in the course of the day. Many are probably liars, busybodies, jealous, and so on. Understanding that the world is full of evil people is crucial. This way, you will be prepared whenever things get out of hand.

You should also spend some time reflecting on the coming day. Always look on the inside and examine yourself. Think about the prior day and the things that you managed to overcome. Did you encounter any challenges? How did you respond to situations? Do these things the minute you wake up and sometimes do it before sleeping.

Always Be Time Conscious

We have to constantly keep in mind that we have very limited time on this earth. Yet our time is quite limited. With each passing day, our mind ages, our skin dies, our relationships fizzle out, and our bodies breakdown. Time is always in motion, and with each tick of the clock, we lose precious moments that will never be recovered.

If you pay close attention to each day, you will realize that we have a tendency to postpone matters that are of utmost importance to us. We need to learn from Marcus Aurelius. Each night he spent some time decompressing. He wrote down the events of the day and thought of how to perform better next time. Learn how to prioritize the most important things and then accomplish these first. Then proceed to accomplish all other things in order of importance. This way, you will have conquered procrastination.

Spend some time each day thinking about the things you have to do and accomplish. As a trader, you have to come up with a trading plan that will include lots of things, such as developing a trading strategy. You will need to determine which trades to enter, which stocks to choose, and amounts to allocate to each trade. It is imperative that you pause and think about these things, as you will be able to critically analyze each step.

Think about the bad or negative things that could happen and then start thinking about all the positives. Pay attention to how you want things to work out for you. What steps can lead to a positive outcome? Think about these steps and focus on them.

If your focus is on the positive and you follow this up with action, then you will stand a much better chance of success than focusing only on trade. A lot of traders and even experts believe trading is all a matter of instituting strategies and has nothing to do with mental toughness.

This is really wrong and misadvised. Trade practices have a huge mental impact on traders. So many traders are confused, worried, and concerned, especially at the prospect of losing money and losing out on different trades. At the first sign of loss, some traders tend to run. They withdraw their funds and cancel trades. This is so wrong because the markets travel in both directions.

Some strategies may go wrong, even with the best planning. As such, traders should not despair. Stoicism teaches us to understand that any situation is not even close to being the worst situation possible. Compare losing some money trading with getting an incurable disease such as cancer. It could be worse, such as contracting a serious viral disease, dying in a plane crash, or even drowning in the sea.

Choose Not to Be Harmed

According to the Stoics, there is no bad or good but only perception. This means that all things happening to us are neither good nor bad. All that is simply a matter of perception, and that is within our control. As such, we should take charge and control perception.

If your initial perception of loss was that it is a bad thing, then you can always go back and change your thinking to view every aspect of trading in a positive manner. You can think of any losses you make as a learning experience and a great opportunity to better your trading skills. Therefore, you will no longer fear trading or even fear losing. Instead, you will have an all-round experience where winning is viewed positively, and losing is also viewed positively.

Also, remember that Stoics spend a lot of their time focusing on their lives and how they can do better in everything they do and how they can be useful to those around them. This means being happier and addressing any issues that you may be facing. Challenges viewed from this aspect cease to be daunting and remain positive endeavors worth tackling.

Day Techniques to Understand the Graphs

Charts are used by traders to monitor price changes. These changes determine when to enter or exit a trading position. There are several charts used in day trading. Although these charts differ in terms of functionality and layout, they typically offer the same information to day traders.

Some of the most common day trading charts include:

1. Line charts
2. Bar charts
3. Candlestick charts

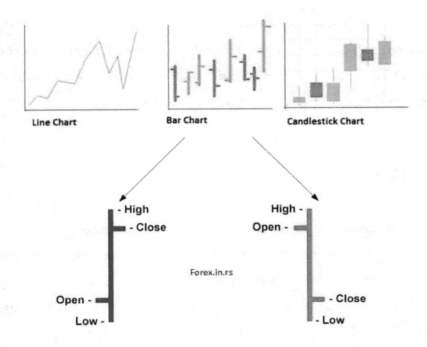

Line Chart   Bar Chart   Candlestick Chart

- High
- Close

High -
Open -

Forex.in.rs

Open -
Low -

- Close
- Low

For each of the above charts, you must understand how they work as well as the advantages/disadvantages involved.

Line Charts

These are very popular in all kinds of stock trading. They do not give the opening price, just the closing price. You are expected to specify the trading period for the chart to display the closing price for that period. The chart creates a line that connects closing prices for different periods using a line.

Most day traders use this chart to establish how the price of a security has performed over different periods. However, you cannot rely on this chart as the only information provider when it comes to making some critical trading decisions. This is because the chart only gives you the closing price. This means that you may not be able to establish other vital factors that have contributed to the current changes in the price.

Bar Charts

These are lines used to indicate price ranges for a particular stock over time. Bar charts comprise vertical and horizontal lines. The horizontal lines often represent the opening and closing costs. When the closing price is greater than the opening price, the horizontal line is always black. When the opening price is higher, the line becomes red.

Bar charts offer more information than line charts. They indicate opening prices, the highest and lowest prices as well as the closing prices. They are always easy to read and interpret. Each bar represents rise information. The vertical lines indicate the highest and lowest prices attained by a particular stock. The opening price of a stock is always shown using a small horizontal line on the left of each vertical line. The closing price is a small horizontal line on the right.

Interpreting bar charts is not as easy as interpreting line charts. When the vertical lines are long, it shows that there is a significant difference between the highest price attained by a security and the lowest price. Large vertical lines, therefore, indicate that the commodity is highly volatile while small lines indicate slight price changes. When the closing price is far much higher than the opening price, it means that the buyers were more during the stated period. This indicates likelihood for more purchases in the future. If the closing price is slightly higher than the purchase price, then very little purchasing took place during the period. Bar chart information is always differentiated using color codes. You must, therefore, understand what each color means as this will help you to know whether the price is going up or down.

Advantages of Bar Charts

- They display a lot of data in a visual format

- They summarize large amounts of data

- They help you to estimate important price information in advance

- They indicate each data category as a different color

- Exhibit high accuracy

- Easy to understand

Disadvantages

- They need adequate interpretation

- Wrong interpretation can lead to false information

- Do not explain changes in the price patterns

Tick Charts

Tick charts are not common in day trading. However, some traders use these charts for various purposes. Each bar on the chart represents numerous transactions. For instance, a 415 chart generates a bar for a group of 415 trade positions. One great advantage of tick charts is that they enable traders to enter and exit multiple positions quickly. This is what makes the charts ideal for day traders who transact volumes of stock each day.

These charts work by completing several trades before displaying a new bar. Unlike other charts, these charts work depending on the activity of each transaction, not on time. You can use them if you need to make faster decisions in your trade. Another advantage of tick chart is that you can customize each chart to suit your trading needs. You can apply the chart on diverse transaction sizes. The larger the size, the higher the potential of making a profit from the trade.

When used in day trading, tick chart works alongside the following three indicators:

- RSI indicators—these are used when trading highly volatile securities. They help you establish when a particular security is oversold or overbought since these are the periods when stock prices change significantly.

- Momentum—day traders use this together with tick charts to show how active the stock price is and whether the activity is genuine or fake. If the price rises significantly, yet the momentum is the same, this indicates a warning sign. Stocks with positive momentum are ideal for long trades. You should avoid these if you wish to close your positions within a day.

- Volume indicators—these are used to confirm the correct entry and exit points for each trade. Large trading positions are often indicated using larger volume bars, while low positions with little volatility are displayed using small volume bars.

Candlestick Charts

Candlestick charts are used on almost every trading platform. These charts carry a lot of information about the stock market and stock prices. They help you to get information about the opening, closing, highest, and lowest stock prices on the market. The opening price is always indicated as the first bar on the left of the chart, and the closing price is on the far right of the chart. Besides these prices, the candlestick chart also contains the body and wick. These are the features that differentiate the candlestick from other day trading charts.

One great advantage of candlestick charts entails the use of different visual aspects when indicating the closing, opening, highest, and lowest stock prices. These charts compute stock prices across different time frames. Each chart consists of three segments:

• The upper shadow

• The body

• The lower shadow

The body of the chart is often red or green in color. Each candlestick is an illustration of time. The data in the candlestick represents the number of trades completed within the specified time. For instance, a 10-minute candlestick indicates 10 minutes of trading. Each candlestick has four points, and each point represents a price. The high point represents the highest stock price while low stands for the lowest price of a stock. When the closing price is lesser than the opening price, the body of the candlestick will be red in color. When the closing price is higher, the body will be colored green.

There are several types of candlesticks that you can use in day trading. One is the Heikin-Ashi chart that helps you to filter any unwanted information from the chart data, ending up with a more accurate indication of the market trend. Novice day traders commonly use this chart because of how clear it displays information.

The Renko chart only displays the changes in time. It does not give you any volume or time information. When the price exceeds the highest or lowest points reached before, the chart displays it as a new brick. The brick is white when the price is going up and black when the price is declining.

Lastly, the Kagi chart is used when you want to follow the direction of the market quickly. When the price goes higher than the preceding prices, the chart displays a thick line. When the price starts to decline, the line reduces in thickness.

Each of the above charts works using a time frame, which is represented using the X-axis. This time frame always indicates the volume of information represented by the chart. Time frames can be in the form of standard time or in the form of the number of trades completed within a specified period as well as the price range.

Charting Software

Each of the above charts is created and viewed using specific software. This can be found in a brokerage firm, although you may also purchase this online depending on the type you want to use.

The software helps you identify the right opportunities by indicating when and how you should start and close positions. They always display the necessary patterns required to estimate future changes in stock prices. Using stock patterns, you can also establish continuations as well as reversals in the stock prices.

Chart software is available in many forms. You may find those that are in the form of mobile apps or others that are web-based. Getting the right software enables you to generate correct charts. This explains why you also need to incorporate technical analysis in your trades.

Most day trading chart tools available are free of charge. Some have a forum where you can learn from experienced traders as you use them. They also come with demo accounts that enable you to master day trading techniques before investing your capital in the business.

Preparation for Day Trading

All over the world, stock markets open in the morning. Those day traders who think they can start trading while munching on their breakfast, with no preparation, are among those who make losses. All businesses open in the morning. No successful businessman just gets up, yawns, and starts his business activities. Successful professionals arrive in their office with a clear idea of how they will tackle the work and related challenges. Likewise, to succeed in day trading, one must prepare beforehand. These preparations include many aspects, such as mental, physical, emotional, and financial.

Professional traders have clear advice for day traders; never trade if you are tired or stressed; never trade if you are feeling highly emotional, and trade with clear money management concepts. Day trading is a sophisticated business activity, where people try to earn money by using their intelligence. Therefore, physical or emotional stress can cause harm to your trading business. You will not be able to make rational decisions if you are tired or feeling stressed.

Before you start the day's trading, you should be physically, mentally, and emotionally alert. A good night's sleep is necessary for traders to tackle the roller coaster ride of stock markets. Here are some steps that will help you prepare for day trading with a cool temperament and calm mind.

Before going to sleep, keep your trading plan ready. Note down the important support and resistance levels. Then mentally go over this chart and imagine how you will trade in the next session in different trend conditions.

Do not spend too much time watching the news about stock markets or anything else. Watching the news may create doubts in your mind about stock trends and influence your decision-making power for the next session. If possible, do some breathing exercises or meditation before going to sleep, which will sharpen your focusing power and reduce stress.

Also, prepare your money-plans for the next trading session. How much will you invest? What will be your loss tolerance level? And what will be your profit booking point? During the trading hours, these decisions have to be made in a split second, and if you are already prepared, you will not hesitate to make the right decision. These will also help you set your goals for intraday trading. Just stick to your goals and you will not face any decision-making problems during the trading hours.

The final stage of your preparation will be an hour before the markets open in the morning. This is the time when you check the news reports about the business and financial world, and the economic calendar. By doing so, you will know what events could influence that day's trading pattern in the stock market. You can also check how the world markets are trading in that session. Sometimes all markets trade in one direction, which will be beneficial to know before your local stock markets open.

Planning for Trading

In day trading, financial instruments are bought and sold within the same session. Sometimes more than once through the same day. To be successful in this endeavor, traders need to know where the price might make important moves. Technical charts are very helpful tools in deciphering this price moment. Anybody involved in stock trading relies heavily on stock charts, which is why successful traders always create their trading plans before making any trading decisions.

When you create a trading plan, you are creating an 'assistant' to help you during the trading hours. This assistant will have all the information you will need for day trading, such as trade entry, trade exit, profit booking, stop loss, and major price moments. Nobody goes looking for a treasure trove without any map. Likewise, no trader worth his or her salt will trade without a trading plan. Let us look at how a trading plan is created:

A trading plan is based on research, takes time, but saves a lot of effort and precious money during the trading hours. It is one of the most essential tools required for success in day trading. Every day trader has heard this saying 'fail to plan, and plan to fail.' Professional traders don't tire of emphasizing the importance of a trading plan. If you take their advice and prepare a trading plan before the markets open, you are halfway through to successful trading.

A trading plan is prepared before markets open and so, it is open to revisions and changes after markets start to trade and price changes. Every trader has a different trading style and based on that, his trading plan could differ from others. But every trading plan must have a few essential details. These are:

1. Major support and resistance levels: One must mark the major support and resistance levels on the trading chart because these will symbolize the trade entry and exit points. These levels should be visible on charts to help in decision making during the chaotic trading hours.

2. Trade entry rules: Your trading plan should include when and why you will enter a trade. This could be a detailed explanation like 'if the price goes above X level, then buy.' Or it could be just a green arrow pointing to that price level.

3. Trade exit rules: Like the trade entry point, mark a trade exit or profit booking points on your trading plan. You must follow these rules meticulously; otherwise, these will become useless, if you plan and do not follow them.

4. Money management rules: Some traders like to note down on their trading plan, how much money they will invest in the next session. They keep checking their profits and losses through the session, and if the day's loss reaches its threshold, they stop trading. This is a good example of money discipline while trading because, in the excitement of trading, one can lose sight of what is happening with the investment capital.

These are the most basic rules to include in the trading plan. As you gain experience and get a hold of trading patterns in stock markets, you can expand your trading plans and include more trading rules in it. But always remember, these rules must be followed. A trading plan is based on research about markets, so every rule is important. Breaking any rule will be like going against the market, which is always harmful to any trader.

Chart Reading & Candlestick Charts

Day traders use different charts for technical analysis. The main types are line charts, bar charts, and candlestick charts. Some Forex traders also use Heiken Ashi and Ranko charts, but candlestick charts remain the most favorite of traders. The cause of this popularity is its simplicity. A green candlestick shows a positive price movement, and a red candlestick signals a fall in price. Day traders use various candlestick patterns to decipher the market trend.

The candlestick charts are more than a hundred years old. These were first used by Japanese rice traders to document the rise and fall in the rice prices. It was such an accurate system that stock traders also adopted it and it has since been a popular chart creating tool.

A single candlestick has two main parts; a body and a tail or wick. The body of the candlestick shows the opening and closing levels, while the wick shows the high and low marks. A green body shows that the price opened low but closed higher. And a red body shows higher open, but lower closing in that time frame. A single candlestick can be assigned to different time frames, ranging from one second to one month. These candlesticks make various patterns on charts. Traders try to decipher the price moment by how long the wick or the body is and how every candlestick is placed with other nearby candlesticks.

Candlestick charts are also used for automatic or algorithm trading, where buy and sell signals are generated by various patterns formed by candlesticks.

The up and down movement in stock prices creates candlesticks on charts. Sometimes, a single candlestick can indicate a trend reversal from high to low or low to high. These are called engulfing candlesticks and are so large that they completely engulf the preceding candlestick. These can be both bullish and bearish candlesticks. A bullish candlestick is formed when the price-move creates a big positive or green candlestick, which overshadows the preceding one. It signals that the price is ready to move higher and to start an uptrend.

Its opposite is a bearish engulfing candlestick pattern. Here, the stock price makes a big red candlestick overshadowing the preceding one. This signals big selling pressure and shows that the price will fall further.

Another popular form of a candlestick is "Doji." Usually, this candlestick forms near the top or the bottom, after the price has made a long moment in either direction. In a Doji candlestick, the body is tiny, and the wicks are long. A small body denotes uncertainty in buyers and sellers, which shows that the market cannot decide whether to go up or down. Such an uncertain signal on top may indicate a trend reversal, and traders prepare for a fall in the market. A Doji formation at the bottom signals that the downtrend may come to an end and traders look for confirmation of a price-rise from lower levels.

Candlesticks create many types of patterns on a technical chart. This could involve a single or two or more candlesticks. There are many books about candlesticks and how to read candlestick charts. Traders who wish to know more about these charts can read some of those books and enhance their knowledge.

Manage Your Time Effectively

Day trading is a demanding profession and requires significant time. Any market session runs for at least 6 hours a day, and you will have to spend that much time watching and observing markets, even if not reading. Apart from trading hours, a day trader needs to research, create trading plans, and keep learning new things. All these require time and effort.

Therefore, to succeed in day trading, you will need to manage your time effectively. Usually, people want to adopt a day trading career so they will have working flexibility. This means freedom from getting up early and rushing to get caught in the morning traffic, freedom from having a boss, and of course, financial freedom. Nothing comes easy in this world. A dream life also requires putting in lots of effort. Many day traders find it difficult to complete their trading routines, such as after-hours research and planning. Part-time traders who are already busy with some other work also struggle to prepare for day trading in their spare time.

With just a few adjustments, a day trader can find enough time to complete all steps required for a successful day trading.

The Beginners Guide

Common Terms

Day trading mechanisms are essential to understand for beginners, and unfortunately, they are also confusing. Knowing and understanding the lingo is important because different things are called by different names. Some of the terms that are commonly used in day trading include:

- Ask – this is the price the seller wants to sell at

- Bid – it is the price a buyer is willing to buy at

- Breakouts – this is when a stock breaks above its preceding level where it was resisted

- Candlesticks – this is a kind of chart where a candle is used to indicate the highs, lows, open and close for any particular period

- Covering – this is the act of buying back shares that were shortly sold

- Float – this is the volume of shares that have been released for the public to trade

- Gap Up/Down – when opening the market, a stock opens above or below the closing price of the preceding day

- Going Long – buying stocks with the aim of selling it at a higher price

- High/Low Day (HOD/LOD) – the price of a stock at its highest or lowest

- Hard to Borrow – a stock not readily available for short. Most often, brokers will charge extra fees to individuals that want to short hard to borrow stocks

- Low Float – this is a stock with low volume in shares that have been traded publicly and experiences high volatility often

- Market Markers – these are entities that facilitate buying and sell orders and are responsible for maintaining liquidity in the market

- Market Cap – this is the dollar value of a company that is subject to its stock prices and remaining shares

- Outstanding Shares – this is the total volume of shares issued. They include the float and institutional ownership

- Profits and Losses (P&L) – the gains and losses of a portfolio over a given period

- Red to Green and Green to Red – this is the movement of a stock from being up on a day to low on the day with the reverse being true

- Resistance – this is the price level of a stock where sellers overpower buyers causing a challenge in increasing the price of the stock

- Scalp – this is where a trader takes advantage of small price movements or changes

- Short selling – this is when a trader sells shares of a stock that he doesn't own while hoping to buy the same shares at a reduced price

- Spread – this is the difference in price between the ask and the bid

- Support – this is the level of price where buyers overwhelm sellers making it difficult to have the shares at a lower price

- Technical Analysis – this is the process of examining the price action of a stock by the use of technical indicators and charts to give a prediction of movements in the future

- Trend – this is the general direction where the price is moving of a particular stock. It can take an upward or a downward trend

Leverage

When it comes to stock trading, you tend to trade with a cap on leverage of two to one. You must have some requirements on the ground before this can be done. Not every investor ends up being approved for that margin account, and this is what a trader needs to be leveraged in a typical stock market.

When it comes to Forex trading, the entire system is totally different. Before you can trade using leverage, you need to have opened the Forex trading account. That's the only requirement that is out there, nothing else. When you open a Forex account, you can easily use the leverage feature.

If you are trading in the United States of America, you will be restricted to a leveraging of 50:1. Countries outside of the US are restricted to leverage of about 200:1. It is better when you are outside the US, than in the US.

If you looked at the $890.67 return in the example above and wondered if there was a way to juice up your returns, then understanding how to use leverage to bolster your returns will help. Just understand leverage, it works both ways. It can magnify your gains and losses.

Let's say you started with $10,000. Your broker may allow you to open what's known as a "margin account." Now, you can buy a stock, without paying for it completely. This is a separate account from your "cash" account, which is the account you would normally buy stocks from. It's not unusual for a brokerage to allow a 50% margin. This means the investor puts up half the cost of the stock purchase, and the broker loans the buyer enough to cover the other 50%. As you would expect, the broker will charge you interest for the use of its money. Keep in mind, the longer you borrow the money, the more interest you'll pay, and if that accrued interest accumulates, you may face higher interest rates as a result. Buying "on margin" works really well when you buy low and sell high. Since you were able to buy $15,000 worth of stock while only putting up $1,000 of your own money, you get all the increased value (minus trading commission and interest) of the investment and not just the increased value of your $10,000. The reverse all occurs if the stock goes down in value. Let's look at both scenarios.

You put $10,000 on the line, and your broker buys you $15,000 worth of XYZ stock. A week later, you sell the stock for $20,000. While this would be described as a $5,000 gain in value ($20,000 − $15,000), but from your perspective, it's actually a $10,000 gain, since only $10,000 of your money was involved. You still have to pay your trade commission ($5) and the interest on your margin loan. Let's say your margin fee is 5%. You will end up paying 5% of the amount borrowed multiplied by the number of days you have kept the shares multiplied by three divided by 360. In our example, this would be $5,000 x 5% x 7 (days)/360 = \$250 x .0195 = \$4.95 plus \$5 commission. Your profit ends up being \$10,000 − \$9.95 or \$9,991.05. That's a pretty nice return on your initial \$10,000 investment!

Your increased investment power has magnified your gain significantly. Unfortunately, the reverse can also happen. Buying on margin can generate losses that can be greater than your initial investment. Margin purchases face other potential problems as well. For a start, the federal government regulates how much margin a brokerage can provide and an investor can use. While it's 50% at the time of this writing, it can change. If you are holding stocks on margin and the fed reduces the maximum marginal rate, you will have to come up with enough money to make up the difference. For example, let's say the fed lowers the margin maximum of 40%, then you are only allowed to borrow \$4,000 on margin, instead of the \$5,000 you and your brokerage originally agreed to. You are now subject to a "margin call." In other words, your broker may contact you and request additional money to make up the deficit. Another event can also trigger a margin call; the value of your stocks goes down. Your broker will have a "maintenance margin" requirement. It varies, for our examples, let's use 50% of the value of the original position.

You've invested \$10,000 of your own money in the stock, plus \$5,000 on margin when the company's shares were selling at \$100 per share, ending up with 150 shares of stock. A week later, the price of the individual shares has fallen to \$50 a share, triggering a margin call. Since your 150 shares of stock are now only worth \$7,500, the equity in a margin account has dropped from $10,000 to $2,500 ($7,500 stock value – $5,000 equity in a margin account after margin loan is subtracted). Since 50% of $15,000 is $7,500, your broker is probably going to ask you for another $5,000 to bring your account back above the maintenance margin. You may have noticed my use of qualifying words ("may," "probably"). This is because your broker is not required to ask you for more money, he has the option of selling as much of your stock holding as needed to bring your position back in line with requirements. He is not even required to tell you he's doing this.

Arbitrage

Sometimes, a trader can take advantage of the inequities of the various financial markets. Suppose you can borrow $100,000 at 5% interest from a bank here in the United States and then loan that money for 10% interest in another country's bank? You would be able to make the 5% interest on money that isn't even yours. You are assuming some risk, though. The bank you're loaning the money too, may not be as stable as the banks here in the United States. If it defaults on your loan, you're on the hook for that money.

An alternative approach is to take advantage of the inefficiency of financial markets. Suppose you buy a stock in a Japanese company on the Tokyo stock exchange that's selling for $10 a share, knowing that the same stock was listed on the New York Stock Exchange for $15 a share. You'd be able to sell your shares for a profit of $5 per share minus commission simply because the New York Stock Exchange was not up-to-date on the value of the Japanese company. (This is kind of an extreme example. Major stock exchanges work very hard to prevent this kind of thing from happening.) Still, arbitrage opportunities do occur. If you pursue one, be careful to calculate the transaction costs carefully. If they are greater than your arbitrage advantage, you will lose money.

Step by Step Instructions of Beginner Day Traders for a Successful Trade

Building up Your Watch List

The first step when you are ready to get started in day trading is to do some research. When you first wake up in the morning, look over your notes and your research and then use that information to create a good watch list. This watch list can be important because it can limit you down to just a few options that you plan to use for trading on that day. There are thousands of stocks on the market and making this watch list will make it so much easier for you to pick the right stocks to invest in.

There are various methods you can use to create this watch list. But one of the best options is to use a scanner. These scanners can look for specific criteria that you want out of a stock and can make things faster than trying to look through them all on your own. To make the scanner work, you just need to list out the requirements that you want the stock to meet and then the scanner will alert you as soon as it finds one that meets these.

Decide Which of These Stocks Work Best for You

After the scanner has given you a few options for stocks that meet your requirements, you can decide which of these the best stocks are. You may have a specific strategy that you would like to go with and then choose the stock that seems to be following that strategy the best. You can always change strategies from one day to the next, or you can choose to stick with one strategy if it is serving your purpose.

Some professionals wait even longer than these five minutes for the market to settle down. There can be a ton of commotion and crazy ups and downs in the market during those first few minutes and investing at this time can hurt your profits. If you spend time looking at your scanner and then investigating the stocks that you receive, it will probably be at least five or more minutes before you are ready to enter the market anyway, but it is still important to be aware of this volatility and learn how to avoid it.

Put That Entry and Exit Strategy in Place

Now that you have a few stocks that are ready to go, you're probably excited to get into the market and start doing your trading. Before you make that purchase, you need to finish up your strategies. This isn't just the overall strategy but also the center and the exit strategy, so you know how to get into and out of the market at the right times.

The first strategy you should work with here is your entry strategy. This is the place where you are comfortable and will purchase your stock. Your aim is to get this entry point as low as you can so that you don't spend too much money and to increase your profits later on. When you look through the charts for that stock, you should be able to find out a safe entry point that will provide you with a reasonable price on that stock.

You also need to come up with an exit strategy. It is important to have a stop for losing money and one for earning money. First, let's look at the stop to losing money. There are times when the strategies that you pick or the decisions that you make are not going to turn out how you wanted and the stock may start to lose money. The point of this stop is to ensure that you can control how much money you will lose in the process. Once the stock ends up reaching this number, you will withdraw from the market, no matter what the stock does later on.

Without this stop, you could end up with a little bit of trouble. Many new traders see that the stock is going down, and they keep riding it out. They hope that the market will turn around. Sometimes the market will turn around, but then there are times when the market will stay low or keep going down.

Purchase the Stocks You Want

After you created your watch list and came up with your enter and exit strategies to keep you safe, it is time to actually go into the market and make your purchase. You will want to have all the criteria in place for that stock before doing this. But if you are working with a strategy, that is going to outline the criteria for you, so just follow that.

If you plan to work with your broker when doing day trading, you would just give them your order to get the trade started. The order is going to include a ton of information that can help the broker do everything that you want. This would include information on which stocks, in particular, you want to purchase, how many shares of each you want to purchase, how much you will spend on these stocks, when you want to enter the market, and when you want to exit the market. The broker is then able to take that information and place the order for you in the system.

There is also the option for you to do all of the work on your own. This is fine to do, but most beginner traders are not going to pick this option because they worry about messing things up or doing something wrong.

Pay Attention

You will quickly find that day trading has some differences compared to other stock trading options. Many other options are longer-term; you purchase the stock and then ride out the market, hoping that your choice will go up over some time. But with day trading, you are only letting the trade occur in one day. The purchase of the stock, as well as the sale of it, all need to happen sometime between open and close of the same day.

This does make day trading a riskier option to work with compared to some of the other stock trading options. This means that you need to really want the market and make some quick decisions on when to buy and sell your stocks. If you don't watch the market, then how are you going to be able to make these quick changes when needed?

As a day trader, you get to focus on watching these ups and downs that occur during the day. This can make it easier to know when you should purchase a stock in the first place and then it helps you to find out when you can sell the stocks to make the biggest profits, or to keep your losses to a minimum.

Once you enter into a trade, you need to pay attention to the market and there may be times when the market changes quickly and you will need to make some quick changes to your position, or close it out, to help you earn more profits or keep the losses down as much as possible. Day trading is not one of those methods where you can place the order and then walk away. If you don't have the time to sit and closely watch the market, make sure to not place an order until you have more time.

Sell Your Stocks When They Reach Your Original Exit Points

It is a good idea to listen to your exit point not only when the market is going down but also when the market is going up. Some people understand why they should follow the exit strategy when the market is going down and they do not want to end up losing too much money in the market. It is a bit harder on them when the market is going up. They may have placed a stop for how much profit they wanted to make, but then they see the market still goes up and they do not want to get out at that time.

While it may be hard, make sure that you are listening to your exit strategy, even when the market is going up. Sure, the market may go past that point, but then it may hit a sharp downturn and you could lose all of that profit. This is another method in place to ensure that your investment stays safe. If the market continues to do well and keeps going up, you will be able to jump back in later on.

Take Some Time to Reflect on That Trade and Write Down Some of the Information as Research Later

As a beginner in the day trading world, there are a lot of things to learn about the market. This is even truer if you have never invested in the past. As a trader, it is your job to learn as you go and make some changes if it is needed. But when you are learning a lot of strategies and keeping track of a large number of trades that are done in day trading, it can be hard to remember everything over time.

Getting a journal and writing down some of your mistakes, your tips, and more after each trade can make a difference.

You don't have to write down a lot of information unless you want to. Just have a few lines or a paragraph. This may seem like it wastes your time. But if you ever get stuck on a trade later on, or if you are trying to find out why you are in a slump and not getting the profits that you want, looking back through this information can make a big difference in how things go in the future.

Startup Your Second (And Third and Forth and So On) Trade

Day trading moves very fast. It is likely that your first trade can be done in a few minutes, though, as a beginner, it will probably take a little bit longer to finish. If there is still time left in the day when you finish up that first trade, then go through these steps again and complete the next trade. Day traders earn a big profit simply by doing a bunch of little trades.

The more of these successful trades that you can get into one day, the more profit you will make. Simply ensure that you are following the same steps that we talked about above and take the same precautions that you did with your first trade.

There are times when you are going to get into the day trading market and you will make a bad trade in the morning. It may not have gone your way, you may have tried to switch your strategy part way through, or maybe you let your emotions get in the way. If the trade was really bad and you feel upset about it, then it is best to just call it good and take a step away from the market for the rest of the day.

The Basic Tips for Beginner's Day Trading

It's time for you to look at how the day trading process works. You could just blindly jump in, but that is a recipe for disaster. Instead, let us get you started on how to smartly engage in day trading.

The first question to ask yourself is, how big an investment are you planning on making your day trading efforts? You need to think that not only how much money you are willing to invest, but also how much time. Many investors look at day trading as an escape from their normal jobs, others see it as an answer to the uncertainties of the job market. While you may hunger to day trade full time, people do succeed as part-time day traders while working a primary job.

Beginners may also want to spend some time simulating investments to get a feel for how comfortable you are with the process and how much talent you may have. Simply jumping in is not a good idea. You need to understand the investment market, learn to look for indicators that give you an idea of stock movements and make the most of your opportunities.

Infrastructure Concerns

While it may sound mundane, spending some time on your workspace and technology can be well worth it. Day trading can be stressful, so a work area that provides quiet and privacy can be helpful. Do not underestimate the importance of a reliable internet connection and a backup method of controlling your investments in case your network goes down. These days, it is not hard to have a fast land-based internet connection while also having the ability to use your smartphone as a wireless hotspot if your main connection goes down. It only takes one network failure when you have a big investment on the line to convince you of the importance of a backup internet access plan.

Understanding the Market

It's one thing to say you want to invest in stocks. It is another thing to find out what stocks you should be investing in. Investors break down the market into different sectors, such as "retailers," "manufacturers," "utilities," "airlines," "energy," "health care," and others. Day traders can choose to target all these sectors or choose to specialize in one or more. As a beginner, focusing on one sector may be advantageous, particularly if it is one you are already familiar with.

Since as a day trader, you are interested in identifying opportunities for small changes in stocks, not long-term growth. This means you will need ample funding. U.S. based day traders need a minimum of $25,000 for their trading account, according to Securities and Exchange Commission (SEC) rules. This means you will really need at least $30,000 to have some flexibility. Keep in mind; in the U.S., you can currently leverage your trading capital up to 400%. This means that you could control $120,000 worth of stock with your $30,000. As you learned earlier, this also means you could suffer four times the losses on your investments. Be aware that if you do not maintain your maintenance margin amount, you can receive a margin call too. In planning for your trading account, it would be better to have more funds available, since that would make more stocks available for your consideration. Remember, it is usually more cost-efficient to buy shares in multiples of 100, meaning a small investment kitty will either limit you to cheaply priced stocks or buying stocks in smaller increments than being less cost-effective too. If you can devote more funds to your trading account, you will be able to pursue more opportunities and have the wherewithal to recover from losses.

Calculating a Simple Moving Average

The moving average is a basic tool to invest or use to monitor a stock's behavior over a defined period. The investor simply adds the stock's closing price for a specific period (two weeks, a month, a quarter, etc.) and then divides that number by the number of trading days in that period. A trader will calculate a short-term moving average and a long-term moving average for a stock (actually, you will probably calculate a few more than this to get a better sense of the stock's behavior). A simple moving average can tell you whether a stock is on a rising or declining trend.

An important point for many traders is when the short-term moving average rises above or below the long-term moving average. A short-term moving average that crosses above a long-term moving average often indicates the stock is about to begin an upward trend. The opposite is also true.

One approach to using moving averages compares a specific short-term moving average (50 days) with a specific long-term moving average (200 days). If the 50-day average moves below the 200-day average, you have a bearish signal. This is known as the "Death Cross." If the 50 average moves above the 200-day average, it is a bullish signal and is known as a "Golden Cross." While it would be nice if you could rely solely on such a simple system, remember that relying only on a moving average approach is unreliable. It is better to use this information as another bit of information when making your trading plans.

Choosing a Broker

Once you have decided on your trading allocation, you need to choose a broker or brokerage. There are several online discount brokers available to the novice investor. Many will offer you their own electronic trading program. Do not be surprised to get offers for free trades and a bonus for picking their firm. Free trades and cash bonuses are nice, but make sure you choose a broker you feel comfortable with and one that checks out with your research.

The biggest online brokerages include TD Ameritrade, Scott Trade, Fidelity Brokerage, Charles Schwab, Options Express, Merrill Edge, Robinhood, Loyal3, Options House, EOption, and others. Some like Robinhood offers free trades, making their overhead on charging interest on margin accounts and using customer cash to earn interest. Others may offer more services or access to more investment exchanges. One thing you will not get from any of these discount brokerages though, is personal advice. That is the purview of the traditional broker.

In choosing a broker, consider the cost of trades, your comfort level with its trading program, and your ability to access the company's website. Furthermore, investigate what others are saying about the brokerage and whether it handles the investment vehicles you are interested in trading.

Buy Orders, Sell Orders, and Setting a Stop Loss Price

Not every move a trader makes must be executed immediately or at random. You can tell your brokerage you only want to buy or sell a stock when it hits a certain price. The risk, of course, is that the stock may not hit that price while you have money planned for it.

You should also plan on setting a "stop-loss price," too. This is a protective move to make sure you do not get badly burned by the stock price moving in the wrong direction. Let us say you bought shares of XYZ Corporation when their price was at $4.50 a share. Based on your research, you expect an upward move by the share price and plan on selling when it reaches $4.75 a share (always have an exit price planned). Then something goes wrong. Bad news upsets the market (in general or it affects your stock in particular), and your stock price starts dropping instead. Wisely, you left a stop-loss order with your broker, in effect instructing the broker to automatically sell your shares when their price drops to a certain point (perhaps in this example $4.35) to limit your loss. You should know that stop-loss orders are not foolproof. Your broker still must find someone to buy the shares at that point. In times of crisis, share prices can fall so fast that they blow by the stop loss price and keep going before they finally sell, making your loss bigger than anticipated. While this is not a regular occurrence, unexpected events can cause them. The company selling the Epi-Pen recently saw its valuation drop $3 billion in a short period of time because of news about its price markup. No day trader could have anticipated this news, and even with stop-loss orders, traders who were expecting upward movement in this stock probably lost more than they expected.

Why Day Trading is the Best Way to Make More Money Investing

Day trading is one of the best methods that you can use to make money in the stock market and with other securities as well. Many people are interested in finding a way that will earn them a good profit, and none will find a better option than day trading. Not like some of the other methods that you can use out there, day trading is unique in that you can start earning profits on your very first day. While other traders may end up having to wait a few months to many years to receive a profit, a day trader is able to get into the market and earn a lot of profits in a short amount of time.

The Best Strategies

The thing to keep in mind is that the best strategy of a day trader is to find something that works and repeat it over and over again.

Once you have decided on that one strategy that works for you, placing an entry, setting a stop loss, and taking a profit, then get on the simulator and practice! That's the way you will work out issues with your strategy. You can go over it as much as you want until you see a continuous profit.

The goal is to be able to control your risk. You want to be able to control your trade risk and your daily risk.

- The quantity you are willing to risk on each trade is referred to as your trade risk. That should ideally be equal to one percent or less of your capital on each trade. You can do that by selecting an entry point and then setting yourself a stop loss. The stop loss will remove you from the trade if the odds go too much against you. You should also learn how to calculate the position size for futures, stocks, and forex because knowing your position size will also help to keep your risk low.

- The amount that you lose in a day is your daily loss. It is smart to set a daily loss limit each day to avoid huge losses to yourself. If you have set your trade loss at one percent, you may want to set your daily risk at three percent. In that instance, you would need to lose three or more trades with zero winners to lose three percent. And if you have practiced using your software and practiced using your strategy, that shouldn't happen often. You want to keep your daily losses small so that on winning days, they are easily recouped.

Trading only two or three hours per day is very common for day traders. However, some do trade for the whole session from nine-thirty a.m. until four p.m., usually for the US stock market. All day traders are consistent in the hours they trade. They trade at the same hours each day, whether they are trading for three hours or the whole session. Here are some of the hours you will want to focus on yourself:

- If you are going to be trading stocks, the best time of the day for trading is the first hour and second hour right after the open, and the last hour of the day before the close. So, between 9:30 a.m. and 11:30 a.m. EST is the first two-hour period you want to find good trades. The biggest price moves and biggest profits are to be had at this time of day. Between 3:00 p.m. and 4:00 p.m. EST is a good hour of the day as well. There are pretty big moves then also, however, if you are going to only trade for two hours in a day, trade in the morning. That's when the market is the most volatile.

- If you will be trading futures, the opening time is the better time to trade. That would be between 8:30 a.m. and 11:00 a.m. EST. Active futures see activity around the clock, so the best trading times are a little earlier than with stocks. Futures markets officially close at different times and the last hour of a contract can also offer sizable moves for you to get in on.

- If you decide to trade the forex market, they trade twenty-four hours a day during the week. The EUR/USD is the favorite of the day traders. It is the most volatile between 06:00 and 17:00 GMT. These are the hours when the day traders should trade this market. The biggest price moves are between 12:00 and 15:00 GMT. This is when both the US and London markets are open, trading the euro and US dollar.

We mentioned before that day, traders find a strategy and then repeat it over and over again. That is what we will talk about now in more detail. These are the basic day trading strategies that are used. There are many others, but these are the most common.

Scalping: Probably, the most common of the strategies is scalping. It is a basic get in there and gets out of there type of mind frame toward trading. Day traders will get in on a good trade and then sell as soon as it starts to show profitability. It's relatively safe and that's why a lot of people like it. You don't watch it and then hope it stays strong.

Daily Pivots: A day trader using this strategy would look to buy their trade at its lowest price during the day and then try to sell it at its highest price of the day. These times are also referred to as low of the day (LOD) and high of the day (HOD).

Fading: This is known as a risky strategy. Day traders will short stocks once they start to gain rapidly. The theory being that the stocks are over purchased and the traders who purchased early will be looking to sell because the stock is gaining and they are making money. The other traders may be scalping. This strategy of fading can be profitable when used correctly, but keep in mind that the risk is higher.

Momentum: If you are a person who would be interested in riding trends, then this type of trading may be a perfect strategy for you. The day traders who enjoy this method watch the current news and are watching for the trends being supported by the highest volumes of trades. Then they jump on the wagon and ride the waves until they see signs of it turning around. Then, of course, they are watching the news releases and they just start all over again.

Stop Losses: The use of stop losses is crucial in day trading. The market is so prone to sharp price movements and you could potentially see substantial losses in a short amount of time if you aren't careful. There are two types of stop losses which we covered earlier. The physical stop-loss order and the mental stop loss. During your whole day trading career, you need to keep these stop losses in the front of your mind.

These strategies that I have given you are not miracle strategies. Just because you master one, it won't make you rich. The main secret lies in consistency. Always be looking at your strategies and evaluating them. Tweak them to work for you by adding other parts of other strategies to them. Use them to find your comfort zone. Find what works for you. It has taken many of the most elite day traders' years to hone and perfect their unique strategies.

If you are to be a successful day trader, aside from reading this book, you must have patience. You may wait minutes to days for a profitable trade to come along. You must be able to make smart decisions. Knowing when to get in and out of a trade is vital. There could be a profitable situation staring you in the face and you have maybe minutes to react. And of course, you must be able to maintain balance. How you react to winning and losing is so important. One day, you can be on cloud nine because the day went perfectly. The next day you could be down in the dumps and depressed because you may have taken a nasty loss. You must maintain balance there for your emotional wellbeing.

How to Become a Day Trader

The following basic tools are recommended:

Computer/Monitor

Well, cheap is expensive. A slow kind of computer can cause you a great fortune. Slow working definitely implies that the day trading tracks to be unreliable and totally not trending. This is really going to charge you in that the rates of profits at the end of any activity will be way low. They can cause you to miss trades, therefore, making your idea so unreliable. Remember, you have a good reputation to uphold.

With all these in mind, please bear a quite fast laptop or monitor.

Set a Target Really Motivating

Setting a realistic trading target is going to manage and monitor your real cash big time. A certain target is put for the purpose of big motivation. Work on that. Be for it big time. Remember achieving your target is normally tough because we all have really "dream" targets. Consistent losses will be incurred too, so prepare to lose some cash. Failure is never good though and will never be, so keep up champ!

Create a Demo Account

Rehearsing has always been a good move as your head to be successful in navigation. Set up a demo account that will help you master all the ropes and moves that are likely to be incurred. Reading the fluctuations, the market trends are one way of future taking master moves that are great chances for high profitability rates. Keep testing and practicing until you are sure that you indeed set to go.

Examine the Market

Master most of the trading moves. This makes you informed and definitely enhances specialization in a particular field.

Fast Internet Connection

A constant, fast, and reliable type of internet connection is highly recommended. The unreliable internet connection can cause a miss in the market trends that can hinder the trading traces in a way leading to major losses being incurred at the end. Most of the users use a cable and ADSL type of connection. Remember that day trading does not recommend any unreliable source of connection.

Type of Market

Choosing the kind of market to start with is super important, choose the most preferred.

Discover the Tax Implications Likely to Be Incurred

Inquire on how taxes revolve around profits. Engage with your financial adviser to let him or her explain how taxes are handled. Are they going to cause a devaluation on the made profits? Are they good news? How does that happen?

Be informed so as to at the end the trader can guess on the likelihood net profits to be expected.

Choose the Right Stocks to Trade

Well, to be better in choosing the right kind of stock, doing some in-depth research on the current existing stock is the first step. Get to know the kind of stocks that are likely to perform well. Most preferably, those that are likely to perform well on a day-to-day basis. Remember to at least try one or two different kinds of stock until you are so sure that you have picked out the right one.

Plan a Good Financial Amount

You will need to have enough on the amount of money that can be risked on the day trading business. It is mostly advised not to risk more than 1-2% of your account money so as to avoid future losses.

Another piece of advice to the beginners, stay away from trading on the margin until you are set with enough moves and good trading wisdom. This will save you some extra cash in time.

Know the Lingo

Becoming an expert clearly requires much effort. There are certain keywords that you are required to be familiar with. Check them out:

- Ask the amount of money a trader is offering for sale.

- Know the bid: This is the money amount a trader is ready to purchase.

- Stock breakouts: Declaring a stock that has experienced a breakout, basically talks of its reduction in the level of resistance.

- Candlestick: This is a type of chart specifically for prices that shows the maximum, minimum, opening, and closing prices for a specified period of time.

- Covering: This refers to the buying back of the trade shares that had been sold earlier to do away with the obligation.

- Float: This is the amount of market share that is ready for day trading.

- Stock Gap Up or Down: This normally occurs when the price of a market trade becomes more or less than its preceding closing price.

- The idea of Going Long: This normally refers to buying a market trade with the objective of offering it for sale at a higher price.

- High of Day and Low of Day: This is the highest or the lowest price a market trade has traded throughout the day.

- Hard to borrow list: This is ideally a list used by brokers that tells the stocks that are hard to borrow for short-term sales.

- Market liquidity: This is a term that describes the state of the market, showing how fast an inventory can be sold or purchased without affecting its price.

- Low Float Stock: This is basically a type of stock with a low number of shares available for trading.

- Market Maker: This term generally refers to any market participant, be it a firm or an individual who can purchase, sell, and clear market trades. A market maker normally operates under given by-laws of a country.

- Market Capitalization: This refers to the overall value of shares and stock of a business center. Most specifically, ordinary shares (unit of capital).

- Outstanding Shares: This is a type of shares that have been given out by a company and have been subscribed by shareholders. They are normally shown as share capital in the company's balance sheet.

- The P&L (Profits and Losses): This is a financial statement, also referred to as an income statement. It indicates the revenue, costs, and expenses incurred by a business for a specified period of time normally a quarter a year.

- Red Green trading: The red and green colors on trading charts also have meaning. The green bar indicates the stock, which is higher compared to the preceding day. The red bar scenario shows the stock, which closed lower that day as compared with the preceding day.

- Resistance: This is the price point of stock, which is normally at a higher level. The price level overpowers buyers, making it hard for the inventory to have a price increase.

- Scalping: Considering every small price ranges that are likely to happen during day trading.

- Short Selling: This activity involves selling off some shares at a price that is likely to make a good profit when buying them later.

- Spread: This is the price bridge between the bids and asks during day trading.

- Support trading: This is a section in a trading chart that indicates where price had dropped and tried it best to break below.

- Technical Analysis: Historical analysis of the price of the stock is involved with the use of mechanisms like charts so as to predict possible outcomes in the future.

- Top trends: This is an actual graphical representation of the stock's movement within trading while monitoring the top trends and downtrends. Trends are so important in day trading because they give the brokers and traders a sense of a particular direction and makes them informed of all moves and plan for better strategies.

Venture Into Several Day Trading Courses to Get Educated

Before getting involved in a particular course of study, kindly consider the following tips:

The course should be taught by a professional

Ignoring his/her profession, just pick out a teacher who happens to be an expert in a specific trading field. Why? So as to acquire detailed, accurate, reliable, and up-to-date pieces of information. This will so motivate you in your trading journey.

Availability of educational support tools

The presence of proper educational tools will give the learner an audience to readily grasp every fundamental piece of information. The professional should also be ready to face time or live chat with any student who really needs great help.

Based on your particular field

Well, we agreed on picking out a particular trading sector field and really working on it. Well, your educational source should go hand in hand in whatever field that you have selected. Make sure that the learning source is detailed so as to acquire a bigger piece of information.

High rated learning the source

A perfectly detailed piece of learning information entails that a lot has been covered. Go for that. We have to make our day trading journeys so well, then meaning that our start-off spots should be good.

Putting all these in mind, take a look at some awesome sources for beginners:

- Books and journals.

- Online courses for day trading.

- Applications or games.

- Beginner level books for day trading.

Perform a Personal Audit

Day trading is much of analytical work. A clear understanding of what is actually going to take place is so needed. Day trading is not a get-rich-overnight thing. It's a step-by-step learning project that involves simple to complex tactics that get to be implemented by the trader during his/her day trading journey.

Set the Right Strategies

First things first, getting to know what you are actually working on is the most important activity. What do I want? How are you going to accomplish all these? Is it worth it? How long is this going to take? What are the possible outcomes?

A little reminder, a proper strategically outline calls for hard work and patience so as to achieve an amazing goal. You got this!

Money Mistakes to Avoid

Now we'll turn our attention to giving some tips, tricks, and advice on errors to avoid in order to ensure as much as possible that you have a successful time trading.

Avoid the Get Rich Quick Mentality

Any time that people get involved with trading or investing, the hope is always there that there's a possibility of the big winning trade. It does happen now and then. But quite frankly, it's a rare event. On many occasions, even experienced traders are guessing wrong and taking losses. It's important to approach Forex for what it really is. It's a business. It is not a gambling casino even though a lot of people treated that way, so you need to come to your Forex business—and it is a business no matter if you do it part-time, or quit your job and devote your entire life to it—with the utmost seriousness. You wouldn't open a restaurant and recklessly buy 1 thousand pounds of lobster without seeing if customers were coming first. So, why would you approach Forex as if you were playing slots at the casino? Take it seriously and act as if it's a business because it really is. Again, it doesn't matter if you officially create a corporation to do your trades or not, it's still a business no matter what. That means you should approach things with care and avoid the get rich quick mentality. The fact is, the get rich quick mentality never works anywhere. Unfortunately, I guess I could say I've been too strong in my assertion. It does work on rare occasions. It works well enough that it keeps the myth alive. But if we took 100 Forex traders who have to get rich quick mentality, my bet is within 90 days, 95% of them would be completely broke.

Trade Small

You should always trade small and set small achievable goals for your trading. The first benefit of trading small is that this approach will help you avoid a margin call. Second, it will also help you set profit goals that are small and achievable. That will help you stay in business longer.

Simply put, you will start gaining confidence and learning how to trade effectively if you get some trades that make $50 profits, rather than shooting for a couple of trades that would make thousands of dollars in one shot, but end up making you completely broke. Again, treat your trading like a real business. If you were opening a business, chances are you would start looking for slow and steady improvements and you certainly would not hope to get rich quickly.

Let's get specific. Trading small means never trading standard lots. Even if you have enough cash to open an account such that you could trade standard lots, I highly recommend that you stay away from them. The large amount of capital involved and margin that would be used could just get you into a lot of financial trouble. For beginners, no matter how much money you are able to devote to your trading, I recommend that you start with micro lots. Take some time and learn how to trade with the small lots and start building your business earnings small profits at a time. Trading only with micro lots will help in force discipline and help you avoid getting into trouble. Make a commitment only to use micros for the first 60 days. After that, if you have been having decent success, consider trading a mini lot. You should be extremely cautious for the first 90 days in general.

Be Careful with Leverage

Obviously, it's extremely beneficial. It allows you to enter trades that would otherwise not be possible. Alternatively, the temptation is there to use all your leverage in the hopes of making it big on one or two trades. You need to avoid using up all your leverage. Remember that you can have a margin call and get yourself into big trouble if your trades go bad.

And it's important to remember there's a high probability that some of your trades are going to go bad no matter how carefully you do all your analysis.

Not Using a Demo Account

A big mistake the beginners make is jumping in too quickly. There is a reason that most broker-dealers provide demos or simulated accounts.

If you don't have a clue what that reason is, let's go ahead and stated here. Brokers provide demo accounts because Forex is a high-risk trading activity. It can definitely be something that provides a lot of rewards and it does for large numbers of traders. However, there is a substantial risk of losing your capital. Many beginners are impatient, hoping to make money right away. That's certainly understandable, but you don't want to fall into that trap. Take 30 days to practice with a demo account. This will provide several advantages. Trading on Forex is different from trading on the stock market. Using the demo account, you can become familiar with all the nuances of Forex trading. This includes everything from studying the charts, to placing your orders and, most importantly, understanding both pips and margin. The fact that there is so much leverage available means you need to learn how to use it responsibly. You need to know how to experience going through the process and reading the available margin and so forth on your trading platform while you are actually trying to execute trades. A demo account lets you do this without risking real capital. It is true that it's not a perfect simulation. The biggest argument against demo accounts is that they don't incorporate the emotion that comes with trading real money. As we all know, it's those emotions, including panic, fear, and greed, which lead to bad decisions. However, in my opinion, that is a weak argument against using demo accounts. The proper way to approach it is to use a demo account for 30 days and then spend 60 to 90 days doing nothing but trading micro lots. Don't worry, as your micro trading lots, you can increase the number of your trades and earn profits. While I know you're anxious to get started, keeping yourself from losing all your money is a good reason to practice for 30 days before doing it for real.

Failing To Check Multiple Indicators

There is also a temptation to get into trades quickly just on a gut level hunch. You need to avoid this approach at all costs. Some beginners will start learning about candlesticks and then when they first start trading, they will recognize a pattern on a chart. Then in the midst of the excitement, they will enter a large trade based on what they saw. And then they will end up on the losing end of a trade. Some people are even worse and they don't even look at the candlesticks. Instead, they just look at the trend and think they better get in on it and they got all anxious about doing so. That means first checking the candlesticks and then confirming at least with the moving average before entering or exiting a position. You should also have the RSI handy and you may or may not want to use Bollinger bands.

Use Stop Loss and Take Profit Orders

Well, I hate to repeat myself yet again, but this point is extremely important. I am emphasizing it over and over because it's one of the tools that you can use in order to protect yourself from heavy losses. One of the methods that you can get out of having to worry about margin calls and running out of money is to put stop-loss orders every time you trade. This will require studying the charts more carefully. You need to have a very clear idea where you want to get out of the trade if it doesn't go in the direction you hoped. But if you have a stop-loss order in place, then you can avoid the problem of having your account just go down the toilet. Secondly, although the temptation is always there to look for as many profits as possible, in most cases, you should opt to set a take profit order when you make your trade. That way you set as we said, distinct boundaries which will ensure that you make some profit without taking too much risk. The difficult thing with doing it manually is that excitement and greed will put you in a position where you miss the boat entirely. What inevitably happens is people get too excited hoping to earn more profits and they stay in the trade too long. The Forex market changes very fast and so what eventually happens is people that stay in too long inevitably end up with a loss. Or at least they end up missing out on profits.

There is one exception to this point. Some times when there is a distinct and relatively long-term upward trend. If you find yourself, by doing the analysis and determining that such an upward trend is here, that might be an exception to the rule. In that case, you want to try to ride the trend and maximize your profits.

Remember Price Changes Are in Pips

Beginners often make the mistake of forgetting about pips. Remember that pips play a central role in price changes, you need to know your dollar value per pip in order to keep tabs on your profit and losses. This is also important for knowing the right stop loss and take profit orders to execute.

Don't Try Too Many Strategies or Trading Styles at Once

When you are a beginning Forex trader, it can be tempting to try everything under the sun. That can be too much for a lot of people. The most advisable thing to do is to stick with one strategy, so don't try scalping and being a position trader at the same time. The shorter the time frame for your trades, the more time and energy, you have to put into each trade. Scalping and day trading are activities that would require full-time devotion. They are also high-pressure and that can help enhance emotions involved in the trades. For that reason, I don't really recommend those styles or strategies for beginners. For my part and to be honest, it's mine alone, I think position trading is also too much for a beginner. It requires too much patience.

Perhaps the best strategy to use when you're beginning Forex trading is to become a swing trader. It's a nice middle ground, in between the most extremely active trading styles and something that is going to try people's patience, such as position trading. When you do swing trading, you can do time periods longer than a day certainly, but as long or short as you need to meet your goals otherwise. Swing trading also takes off some of the pressure. And it gives you more time to think and react. This does not mean that you can't become a scalper or day trader at some future date.

Next Steps for Beginner Traders

The 7 Essentials for Day Trading

1. Acquire Knowledge

While trading, having the right information is critical in ensuring your trading success. Most people engage in trade with little information and end up regretting their choices after they have encountered losses. You do not have to learn from your own mistakes for you to start doing things right. At times, it is good to learn from others and pick up some lessons without having to experience them on your own. Well, we constantly speak of how powerful knowledge is, but we rarely take time to gain more knowledge. If you have recently started trading, it is important that you learn to embrace learning and gaining the necessary information. There is a lot of learning that you will need before you master the art of trading. In this book, you will find that most of my emphasis is on learning. I know that you cannot go far if you have not mastered what you are doing. For you to succeed, there are a lot of factors that are involved; however, in trading, learning is the most important factor. The difference between a beginner trader and an expert comes in the information that they hold. Most people believe that knowledge goes with years of experience. However, I fail to agree with such beliefs. One can be in an industry for long and fail to learn, and at the same time, one could have recently joined, yet their commitment to learning sets them apart. It all goes with how willing we are to gain knowledge.

You are probably wondering which avenues you can use to learn more about trading. It is amazing that you are already utilizing one of the methods that involve reading books. In the digital world that we are in currently, the internet has been one place where we can derive practically any information. There is a lot of details that we can get from different websites, blogs, journals, and social media platforms. As a disciplined individual, you may decide to spare a few hours of your time learning. You can start small with a few minutes as you advance to gaining more knowledge and applying them to your strategies.

2. Decide the Amount of Capital to Spend

In most instances, we fail to discuss the amount of money we need to spend while trading. The majority of the traders begin trading, not knowing the importance of setting a budget. At times, we engage in more than we can afford or less than we can afford. You would rather spend less than what you have than spend more than you have. Sadly, the majority end up using more than they can afford to lose. As you decide to engage in options trading, it is important that you come up with a budget. The budget is not meant to restrict you, but it is meant to help you avoid making trading mistakes that you will regret later on, especially if a trade does not turn out as you would have expected.

Many traders are consumed in the idea of spending more to earn more, which may not always be the case. You can still earn from a small investment, depending on the strategy that you use while trading. At the same time, you can encounter a loss and lose all the money that you had invested. In such circumstances, it would be better if you made a small investment instead. If you are a beginner, try to avoid starting with a huge investment. Assuming that at that point, you do not know much. It would be best if you started small and later advanced to huge investments.

3. Create a Trading Plan

A plan is essential to a trader since it provides a sense of direction. Having a good plan can help you achieve success while trading, and it can place you in a better position as compared to an individual who lacks a plan. Most of the successful traders will tell you that they had plans that inspired them while trading and helped them scale to a bigger height. Success is not something that comes instantly. We have to properly plan for it and ensure that we have put up measures that can guarantee that we get to the point that we want in life. At times, it is very easy to forget why we started. Thus, we need a plan that shows our goals. Such goals give us something to live for and inspire us to give our best in what we do. In spite of the challenges that we face, we feel motivated to keep pushing and to keep trying. Without inspiration, it is difficult to succeed and to push to greater heights. We get comfortable in situations that we should not get comfortable with, and this results in stagnation. It is about time that we learn to stay out of a limited mentality and learn to expand our thoughts and ideas on how to live best. This brings us in a situation of motivating ourselves to do more in life.

4. Have the Right Trading Strategies

While trading, you need to come up with approaches that can guarantee you trading success. One of the ways to ensure that you become a trading expert is to have the information at the tips of your fingers. In this case, ensure that you familiarize yourself with all the trading strategies that are useful to a trader. At times, this is not the kind of information that you learn in one sitting. It requires commitment and dedication while mastering the art. For some, they learn from the mistakes that they make while trading. You might have utilized a certain strategy that failed to work, and hence, you note the circumstances of the trade and note why the strategy did not work. Documenting such will help you avoid making the same mistake another time. At the same time, you can also learn from strategies that worked through the same formula. After a successful trade, note all of the underlying factors that contributed to your success, and you have to be willing to utilize them another time. Each process involved while trading offers a chance to learn more. As a wise trader, you should be ready to learn at all times and ensure that you are willing to improve at all times. The expedition may not be as smooth as we expect it to be. However, with the will and determination to learn, it becomes possible to achieve the goals that we hold.

5. Have a Mentor

Having a mentor will create a difference in your day trading journey. As an investor, you may have a financial planner or a life coach, but do you have a trading mentor? The same way you invest in having a better life and properly utilizing your earnings should be the same way you invest in trading. It is important to note that day trading is like any investment; hence, you have to place certain mechanisms to ensure that you succeed. Truth be told, trading options is not a walk in the park for all traders. For some, it is difficult to come by all the technical terms involved, and this, in turn, makes the investment to suffer from low or no returns. Ideally, no one engages in an investment with the intention of failing at some point. You mainly aim to become successful in the trades you make for you to be proud of what you have achieved so far. Having a mentor does not mean that you are weak on your own. It means that you are strong enough to acknowledge that you need guidance to grow and move further than where you are currently. It is a brilliant move to have such an acknowledgment. A mentor should help in accelerating the different processes. Basically, if you were to get somewhere with 30 steps, with the help of a mentor, you get there with 15 steps.

6. Set Some Goals

Once you decide to invest in day trading, establish some goals that would motivate you to keep investing regularly. There are certain days when you will feel like you made the wrong decision, and you may be tempted to quit. On some days, your strategies in trading may not move as you would expect, which will make you feel demotivated to push further. Having goals changes the whole mood. They give you something to look forward to. This means that regardless of the challenges that you face, you always feel inspired to do better, and even when you feel like giving up, you find a reason to keep pushing. Waking up every morning, feeling motivated by what you do, may appear to be a hassle for some. You find that it is like you are forcing yourself to get in the mood to succeed, and you are barely making a difference in your life. When you decide to trade, learn to love what you do. The passion that you develop makes the whole process easier and manageable. Most traders are completely uninspired by what they do. Some start trading simply because they need to invest and grow their money. With such an attitude, learning becomes difficult, and it also translates to the results that you get. For instance, you remain at the same point while starting, and you barely make progress. This happens mainly because you are uninspired.

7. Start Small

The biggest challenge with day trading is that most people engage in trade with huge expectations of becoming rich within a short time. We are clouded with the fantasies of earning a fortune overnight, and we end up feeling frustrated when things do not go as we planned. We have to come into terms with the fact that trading is not a "get rich fast" scheme. We know some people who have been fortunate enough to earn a lot within a short period, but not everyone gets lucky. There are some who are still in the same position where they started. This mainly occurs when an individual fails to properly understand the mechanisms involved while trading. Such mechanisms involve trading strategies, trading plans, trading patterns, and how to conduct successful trades. There is no rocket science involve while learning some things. As long as you are committed and willing to learn, there is nothing that can stop you from acquiring the information. You can decide to commit some of your time to learn and sharpen your skills. With time, you master the art and become an expert. In most cases, you find people setting high targets that seem unachievable, yet they anticipate getting to those levels. As a trader, it is important that you set realistic goals. For instance, with a small investment, set an amount that is slightly higher than what you invest in with half profit or slightly more than what you spent.

The Platforms and Tools You Need to Have to Become a Trader

For you to carry out day trading successfully, there are several tools that you need. Some of these tools are freely available, while others must be purchased. Modern trading is not like the traditional version. This means that you need to get online to access day trading opportunities.

Therefore, the number one tool you need is a laptop or computer with an internet connection. The computer you use must have sufficient memory for it to process your requests fast enough. If your computer keeps crashing or stalling all the time, you will miss out on some lucrative opportunities. There are trading platforms that need a lot of memory to work, and you must always take this into consideration.

Your internet connection must also be fast enough. This will ensure that your trading platform loads in real-time. Ensure that you get an internet speed that processes data instantaneously to avoid experiencing any data lag. Due to some outages that occur with most internet providers, you may also need to invest in a backup internet device such as a smartphone hotspot or modem. Other essential tools and services you need include:

Brokerage

To succeed in day trading, you need the services of a brokerage firm. The work of the firm is to conduct your trades. Some brokers are experienced in day trading than others. You must ensure that you get the right day trading broker who can help you make more profit from your transactions.

Since day trading entails several trades per day, you need a broker that offers lower commission rates. You also need one that provides the best software for your transactions. If you prefer using specific trading software for your deals, then look for a broker that allows you to use this software.

Real-Time Market Information

Market news and data are essential when it comes to day trading. They provide you with the most recent updates on current and anticipated price changes on the market. This information allows you to customize your strategies accordingly. Professional day traders always spend a lot of money seeking this kind of information on news platforms, in online forums, or through any other reliable channels.

Financial data is often generated from price movements of specific stocks and commodities. Most brokers have this information. However, you will need to specify the kind of data you need for your trades. The type of data to get depends on the type of stocks you wish to trade.

Monitors

Most computers have a capability that enables them to connect to more than one monitor. Due to the nature of the day trading business, you need to track market trends, study indicators, follow financial news items, and monitor price-performance at the same time. For this to be possible, you need to have more than one processor so the above tasks can run concurrently.

Classes

Although you can engage in day trading without attending any school, you must get trained on some of the strategies you need to succeed in the business. For instance, you may decide to enroll for an online course to acquire the necessary knowledge in the business. You may have all the essential tools in your possession, but if you do not have the right experience, all your efforts may go to waste.

Price Action Strategies

Now let's take a look at some of the strategies that you can employ using price action. Since it's one of the easiest methods, it's very suitable for beginners. Learning to manage your money is one of the most important things that you can do in day trading. Managing your money well is one of the ways you will guarantee yourself a success.

Inside Bar Strategy

As its name suggests, this day trading signal begins with a gap up that will develop into an inside bar so that you then have a setup. If there aren't many stocks opening with a full gap, you may want to consider looking at a stock that is partially gapped up. This will be ok as long as they are above the preceding day's close and below the preceding day's high. So, you have to look at these very carefully. Always do your research, but do it quickly.

So, you have your inside bar. Now you want to place your stop. You want to place it right above the high of the inside bar. Now that you have your stop in place, it is a good time for you to decide where and how you want to exit the trade. If, in the meantime, your stop is hit, then just count it as a loss and move on.

Don't forget. Before you take that trade on, know where you are going to put that stop. Also try to have a clue about your exit.

Gap Up or Gainer Lateral

A gainers list is also known as a percent change list. It is a list of stocks that is kept up-to-date in real-time. They are in rank according to their percent of gain or their net dollar gain from the preceding day. Stocks on these lists are in play. They will get a lot of devotion from traders and will probably have a higher than usual volume.

On these lists, you will be looking for stocks that have formed a lateral. When you find a stock with a lateral, that's when you will enter the trade and immediately place a buy stop above the lateral. Now what you are doing is waiting on a breakout to get a long position in the stock. Should the stock break out and you've bought it, and then make sure you place your stop immediately.

Now is when you need to think about your exit strategy. Know in advance if you are going to use a profit target or not in the trade and how you are going to set the target. This is always something that you should know before the trade is begun. It would be a good idea to plan these things in the morning before you begin trading, depending on the trading you will be doing for the day. Make things easy on yourself at first. After a while, you will get a system in place and quick decisions will come naturally to you.

Gap Up or Gainer Triangle

As with the last strategy (the lateral strategy) you will be looking on the gainer's list or for stocks that have gaped up at the opening of the day. As you are looking at them, you will be looking for a triangle chart pattern. It can be at any angle, symmetrical or ascending.

Just like the preceding strategy, when you see the pattern emerge, you can enter a buy stop order immediately above the triangle, or you can watch for the breakout and then place a stop right below the breakout bar or below the preceding bar.

There are some days where it will feel like your stops are never touched and other days, it will feel like the market is out to get you. Unfortunately, that's just how it will go. But remember that it's part of the process and not to get discouraged or depressed.

Gap Up, Attempt to Fill or Breakout

This strategy is simple and is just as its name implies. It is a stock that has gaped up and is beginning to attempt to fill the gap. And it doesn't matter how much the gap gets filled. The only thing that will matter to you in this strategy is that the stock is attempting to fill.

The stock attempting to fill will require the price to go below the first 10-minute bar. It is also usually a sign that there is a decent supply of traders and they are currently short. They are anticipating the stock to go even lower. So, when that stock does a 360 and moves back into the range of the first 10-minute bar, it makes some of those traders with short positions start to sweat. Why? Because those traders have lost whatever gains they had and are most likely now trying to find out whether or not the stop they placed is going to be hit for a loss presuming that they placed it above the first 10-minute bar.

Now what happens is that the breakout comes in. It's usually fast-paced and because of all the traders, it will be on a higher than average volume. All of those traders that go short squeeze before are now stopped out, so they are coming back in with a new long position, which means that they are fueling the upside breakout even more!

Gap Up or Gainer the Afternoon Breakout

This is incredibly simple. Scan your morning lists in the afternoon. Repeat the same strategies from the morning. Usually, in the morning, there is a strong price rise. Then during the late morning and afternoon, things usually calm down. And this is what you want to see.

In the afternoon version of these strategies, you will want to be looking for the stocks that are just kind of going nowhere. Then watch for one that seems to be inching its way up to resistance. That's when you want to place a buy stop order and watch closely for a possible breakout.

There are, of course, some stocks that won't ever breakout. But that's ok, because there are plenty more to try.

This trading strategy is like an old friend. It's easy to understand and comfortable to be around.

Fibonacci Retracement and Breakout

So far, this will be the most complicated trading strategy. Trading with this method won't even require you to use any indicators after you've become used to it.

Fibonacci Retracement Pattern

Prices move in a 1-2-3 pattern in all time frames no matter what you are trading. No matter if it's stocks, bonds, futures, etc. Every move made is followed by a retracement and then followed by another move up. You may not notice it right away because sometimes it is hidden within a bar on a chart. However, after you study enough charts, you will start learning to recognize it quickly.

The most important thing right now for you to remember is that Fibonacci day trading is centered on .618, which is also referred to as the golden ratio. You can find that ratio by carrying out the Fibonacci sequence far enough and then dividing any number by the number to the right of it. The two most popular Fibonacci retracement ratios are .382 (38%) and .618 (62%). No one knows if they are so important because they are naturally and universally fulfilled or because so many day traders know of them and use them continually, creating a self-fulfilling prophecy.

Fibonacci Retracement Trading Strategy

Looking at a thirty-minute chart, you will be watching for a stock that has made the highest high in the last two days. When doing this, you must have the 15 SMA cross above the 35 SMA on that day.

Then you will be looking to see the price give a retracement back to between 38% and 62% the next morning. If it is a bit over or under, that's fine. It doesn't have to be perfect. Then what you want to see is the price to form a rising bar on the MACD histogram. The whole point is that you want to see a good retracement with some movement back in the direction of the impulsive move.

Once you have seen those things happen, you want to switch to your 10 min chart and watch for your breakout trigger.

Fibonacci Retracement Strategy Signals

The buy Setup: On the 30-minute chart, the price makes the lowest low in two days. The 15 SMA crosses below the 35 SMA on that day. The price has pulled back to the Fibonacci sequence level of 38%-62% and the price also creates a falling bar on the MACD histogram.

Buy Trigger: On the ten-minute chart, the price breakout of a low of the thirty-minute bar that creates the falling histogram bar.

Exit: Price target.

Fibonacci sequence trades are harder to find because they aren't on a list and they don't just fall into your lap. However, once you find them, they can turn into some very nice trades for you.

Gap Down Then Gap Fill Inside Bar Then Breakout

This strategy is a perfect example of a trading technique that takes advantage of other traders caught in a short squeeze who are on the wrong side of the gap.

A lot of day traders, when beginning their career, will quickly grab a stock on the short side when they see it on a gap down list in hopes that it will keep falling for a nice profit.

It may appear backward to go after stocks that have gapped down. However, some short squeeze action can bring them to life quickly and send them soaring like a rocket during the day. We talked about this before when people reverse their position and then the stock moves up much more. If someone gets stopped out of a short position, they have to buy the same number of shares that they shorted to break even. If they switch their position immediately, they are buying twice as many shares. That's how this intraday strategy can really boost a stock upward very quickly. If you can catch yourself on the right side of a few of these during the week, they will certainly make up for a bunch of small losing trades.

Inside Bar Strategy

The inside bar pattern occurs on a chart, on any time frame when the bar's range is completely contained inside of the high-low range of the bar before it. Even just by looking at this pattern is easy to locate on any chart during the day. If you don't feel like searching for it, there is always software that will do the search for you. The inside bar strategy uses multiple time frames to trade intraday from the inside bar pattern formed on a daily chart.

Reduced Volatility

When you see an inside bar on any price chart, it represents an immediate reduction in the amount of price action volatility. Often, they will form after a time of price expansion and higher volatility.

When you see these areas of reduced volatility, they are a gift to alert traders. They are a representation of squeeze points and they offer important support and resistance levels that you can then use to your advantage. They are very important because these areas of squeezed or reduced volatility usually lead to areas of price expansion, and if you are a part of that, you could potentially see significant profits!

Inside Bar Trading Overview

What you want to look for with this strategy is a bar on the inside that has formed on the stock's daily chart at the end of the day. When you find that, put that stock on your watch list for the next day. It is kind of like prepping for the next day or doing your homework. Then the next day, you can watch that stock for a potential breakout of the inside bar's range on a 5- or 10-minute chart. Whichever you prefer is fine. The inside bars are also known as "narrow range bars," and they perform better when using this strategy.

How to Find Inside Bars

You can search for inside bars manually or you can search automatically by scanning the charts with the "average true range indicator." You will set the ATR to 1 day instead of 14 days, which is the normal default. And that will allow you to find the stocks you will want to put on your watch list for the next day easily.

Please keep in mind that the day trading strategies we have gone over here are trade set-ups and not complete systems. They are meant to help you create opportunities to enter trades. You must refine them and add your own stops and exit strategies. Additionally, you will need to decide position sizing for each and every trade that you make.

Whenever you create a system, I would recommend that you test it. You want to make sure that it will have a positive expectancy. You don't want to do the experimenting live on the market using your resources when you find out that your new system isn't up to par.

Also always keep in mind that future market behavior is not going to ever look exactly like the past. So when you are looking at assessment and quantification data, this is something that you may want to remember. We just need to try to adapt it to the existing market as we go along.

Tips for Success

Keep the Risk in Mind

Before you go ahead and make the decision to ultimately pull the trigger on any potential currency trade you are currently considering, the first thing you are going to want is to go ahead and make sure that you know how likely you are to get your money back as well as actually turn a profit. This is why it is always so important to analyze the data that you gather as there is no other way of determining the mood the market is in which means essentially going into a trade just to gamble, and there are better ways to gamble than through the forex market. Additionally, you will want to know when to go ahead, and cut your losses and having a clear idea of the overall level of risk will make this easier to determine as well.

With a clear idea of what sort of risk is going to be required for the trade in question, you will then have more tools at your disposal when it comes time to actually mitigate the risk that you have found, or at least to decrease it as much as possible. Ensuring that the odds of actually turning a profit are in your favor means setting a tight stop loss and not letting your emotions get in the way in the heat of the moment. The point that you start a trade and the point that you set your stop-loss can be considered the maximum amount of risk you are accepting for a given trade.

It is important to always determine the acceptable amount of risk you can handle before you actually make the trade when your emotions are of a nominal concern. If you wait to set a stop loss until after the trade is already in progress, then you run the risk of letting your emotions cloud your better judgment and losing profits in the process. If you feel the need to change your stop loss coming on, then you are going to want to take a moment and consider exactly what it is you are thinking about doing and if it is something that you would consider if you were just getting in at that moment. With a few moment's consideration, your answer should be clear.

To preserve your emotions from getting the better of you, prior to going into each trade, you are going to want to keep in mind the point that you will always get out when you are happy with your profits, no matter what. When it comes to maximizing your profits, a stopping point is just as important as a good stop-loss point. You may be tempted to stay in as long as possible in an effort to squeeze the most profit out of a good trade as possible, but this will lose you more than it will make you in the long run, guaranteed. Instead, the right choice is to cash out half of your holdings and then pick a new point further up so that you protect your profits while also maximizing them.

Finally, regardless of how much of a sure thing a specific trade may appear to be, you need to get in the habit of never investing more than you can afford to lose in a single trade. This means that if you start with $5,000 that you can invest in the forex market, then you never want any single trade to cost you more than $100. This is what is known as the 2 percent rule and it is crucial to remain financially solvent while investing in forex, especially when you are just starting out. While you will likely come up against moments where you want nothing more than to buck this trend, especially when you are riding high on a quality pair, sticking with it is what separates successful forex traders from amateurs. If you can't afford to lose it, don't put it in the pot, it is as simple as that.

Trade With the Right Mindset

If you ever hope to stick around the market long enough to think of yourself as an expert trader, there are several skills you are going to need to become very adept at using. First and foremost, this means always trading with a cool head, no matter what. When you are trading, your goal should be to be as emotionless and robotic as possible. The only thing that matters when you are trading is the numbers and if you worry about anything else while doing so, you are doing it wrong. Trading in the forex market successfully often means having the ability to make split-second decisions, something that just can't be done if you let your emotions get in the way.

Understanding the fact that your emotions are only getting in the way and acting on that fact are two extremely different things. The first emotion that you are going to need to focus on banishing is anger. It can be easy to get angry when a trade that appears as though it is going to be a sure thing suddenly turns sideways, but a more effective use of that time is to instead immediately do what is required to minimize the losses, rather than standing there yelling at them. Aside from anger, the most common emotion that you are likely to come across is going to be fear. It can be easy to become afraid, especially if you broke the 2 percent rule and invested too heavily in a single pair; that doesn't mean it is productive, however, and indeed it can be even more dangerous than anger as it can be paralyzing as well. To stop this from happening, you will need to train yourself to push the emotion aside and act on the facts if you ever hope to find real success in the forex market.

Psychology in Trading

Trading with Emotions

It is common for traders to have their emotions and feelings jumbled up when day trading, from the highs and the lows they experience from the market. This is a far outcry from the confident self that a trader usually poses before the markets open, bubbling up with excitement over the money and profits that they intend to make. Emotions in trading can mess up and impair your judgment and your ability to make wise decisions. Day trading is not to be carried out without emotions, but rather as a trader. You should know how to work your way around them, making them work for your good. A clear level headed and a stable mind should be kept at all times, whether your profits are on the rise, or whether you are on a losing streak. This is not to mean that as a trader, you are to disconnect from your emotions.

Greed

A trader may be fueled to earn more money by checking their balances in their accounts and seeing it be as of a low level. While this may be a motivator to work hard, some traders take it too far, wanting to earn a lot of money right there and then. They make mistakes while trading that has reverse effects than the intended ones...

Taking Unnecessary Risks

Greed for more money will seek to convince the trader to take risks that are not worth so as to achieve a certain financial threshold in the trading account. These will most likely end up in losses. The risky traders may take risks such as high leverage, that they hope will work in their favor, but at the same time may have them making huge losses.

Making an Overtrade

Due to the urge to make more and more money, a trader may extend over long periods of time trading. Commonly these efforts are to naught, for overtrading through the highs and the lows of the market put a trader in a position where their accounts can be wiped off as a result of greed. Not putting into account, the time of trading and plunging into opening up trades without having done an analysis will most likely result in a loss.

Improper Profit and Loss Comprehension

Wanting to earn a lot of money within a short period of time will have a trader not closing a trade that is losing, maintaining the losses, and on the other hand, overriding on profit-making trade until a reverse in the market happens, canceling out all the gains made.

Fear

Fear can work in both directions, as a limit to an over-trade, or also as a limit to making profits. A trader may close a trade so as to avert a loss, the action motivated by fear. A trader may also close a trade too early, even when on a winning streak in making gains, in fear that the market will reverse and that there will be losses. In both scenarios, fear is the motivator, working in avoiding failure and success at the same time.

The Fear to Fail

The fear to fail in trading may inhibit a trader from opening up trades, and just watch as the market changes and goes in cycles when doing nothing. The fear of failing in trading is an inhibitor to success. It prevents a trader from executing what could have been a successful trade.

The Fear to Succeed

This type of fear in trading psychology will make a trader lose out his profits to the market when there was an opportunity to do otherwise. It works in a self-harming way in the market scenarios. Such traders in this category fear having too much profit and allow losses to run, all while aware of their activities and the losses they are going to make.

Bias in Trading

There are several market biases that a trader may tend to make that may be a result of emotions play, which traders are advised against. In the psychology of trading, these biases may influence a trader to make unwise and uncalculated trading decisions that may prove to be loss-making ones. Even when the trading biases are in focus, as a trader, you have to be aware of the emotions in you and come up with ways to keep them in check and maintain a cool head in your trading window.

Bias in Overconfidence

It is a common occurrence with traders, especially new traders, that when you make a trade with huge profits, you get in euphoria in the state of winning. You want to go on opening up trades, with the belief that your analysis cannot go wrong, boiling down to the profits and gains you've made.

This should not be the case. One cannot be too overexcited and overconfident in the analysis skills that you believe you cannot make a loss. The market is a volatile one, and therefore the cards can change at any given time, and when they do, the over-excited and overconfident trader now turns into a disappointing one.

Bias in Confirming Trades

In trading psychology, the bias in confirmation of a trade you have already made, justifying it, is one of the factors that waste a lot of time and money for traders. This type of bias is mostly associated with professional traders. After making a trade, they go back in evaluating and analyzing the trade they just made, trying to prove that it was the correct one, whether they sailed according to the market. They waste a lot of time digging for information that they are already aware of. They could also be proving that the mistake they did in opening a wrong trade and making a wrong move was a correct one.

Bias in Anchoring on Obsolete Strategies

This type of bias in the psychology of trading applies to the traders that rely so much on outdated information and obsolete strategies that do more harm than good to their trading success.

Anchoring on the correct but irrelevant information when trading might make the trader susceptible to making losses, a blow to the traders who are always lazy to dig up for new information on the market. Keeping up with the current events and factors that may have an impact on the market is one of the key aspects of having a successful trading career.

Bias in Avoiding Losses

Trading with the motive to avert losses usually boils down to the factor fear. There are some traders whose trading patterns and their trading windows are controlled by fear of making losses. Having gains and making profits is not a motivation to them when fear hinders them from opening trades that could have otherwise been profitable. They also close trades too early, even when making profits in a bid to avert the losses, their imaginable losses.

Psychology Affecting Traders' Habits

Psychological aspects affect habits in trading, the mistakes, and the winning strategies that a trader comes up with. Explained below are the negative habits that many traders make with the influence of psychology on their habits.

Trading without a Strategy

With no trading strategy and plan, a trader will face challenges with no place to refer to the anticipated end result. A proper strategy should be drawn by a trader to be a referencing point when facing a problem in trading in the market. It should be a clearly constructed plan, detailing what to do in certain situations and which type of trading patterns to employ in different case scenarios. Trading without a strategy is akin to trading to lose your money.

Lack of Money Management Plans

Money management plans are one of the main aspects of trading, and without solid strategies in this, it is difficult to make progress in making gains in the trades opened. As a trader, you have to abide by certain principles that will guide you in how to spend your money in the account in opening up trades and ensuring that profits ensue from that.

Wanting to Be Always Right

Some traders always go against the market, placing their desire of what manner they would like the market to behave in. They do not follow the sign that the market points to, but rather they follow their own philosophy, not doing proper analysis and always wanting to be right.

Remedying the Effects of Psychological Habits

Coming up with Clear Cut Goals

Drawing clear and concise goals and strategies to trade helps a trader in having a vision of trading, and just not doing it for the sake of trading. Writing down goals also works to improve the confidence levels of the trader. Working with a well comprehensive strategy is a profit-making plan in the market.

Setting up Rules for Trading

Rules for the trader work for the good in ensuring discipline in trading. As a trader, you should come up with rules that govern the time of the day that you start trading, the time that you close your trades, and whether or not you trade on a daily basis, or whatever your trading window is. Rules are the backbone of successful trading; when to close a losing trade and at the same time when to close a winning one.

Initializing Money Management Strategies

Coming up with money strategies is not enough, but also actualizing the strategies is equally important.

Money management strategies are of great importance in ensuring that a trader's profitability is put first, putting into consideration the risk of loss. Put the money strategy into action to avoid trading haphazardly and trading with emotions.

Mindset of a Successful Trader

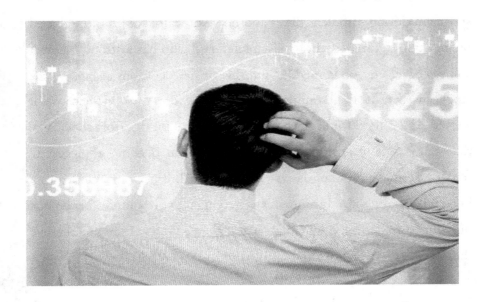

Trading in financial markets can be a bumpy road if you feel that your mental energy is no more and that you cannot focus on the markets anymore. Luckily, you can resolve this problem and start enjoying trading once again by improving your mindset. Some people opine that stock markets are generally immoral, but the fact is that stock markets are neither immoral nor moral. Stock markets lack emotions; that's why it is up to you how you perceive the stock market to behave. If you want to enter the business of the stock market for the long-term and also establish yourself as a full-time day trader, you must develop a specific mindset that aids you in observing the stock market from an unemotional point of view.

It is your mindset that will control your reactions to different transactions. It is your mindset that will help you define how you react to lost trades and big profits. Your mindset will define how you can stay calm during turbulent times and how you can avoid reacting based on emotions. A trader who is disciplined and who has a strong mindset will never let emotions meddle with his or her decisions regarding the stock market. If this sounds hard for you, don't worry because it should sound hard for every beginner. It takes a bit of effort to achieve that status. There is no way by which you can become a successful trader overnight. Trading is just like another business. As you cannot become a successful businessman overnight, you cannot become a disciplined trader overnight. You need to give yourself time to achieve the success that you are looking forward to.

Importance of a Positive Mindset

The stock market is void of emotions, but the participants of the markets are usually full of them. This is the reason reading chart patterns and trends work so well when it comes to trading. They show us some well-known patterns that humans possess. That's how, as a trader, you can take advantage of the market psychology. There is a notorious saying that 90% of traders lose 90% of funds in 90 days. This is wicked, to say the least, but still, this phrase is popular among traders. Before you take the leap in the stock market, you should ask yourself what are the psychological traits that 10% of the remaining traders have. What potentials they possess that make them different from the rest of the lot. If 90% fails, the money they have lost has surely gone to the 10% who succeeded. That's intriguing! Isn't it? When you lose, someone is earning on your money. The people who are earning on your money are humans just like you. They are a small bunch of traders who have found the secret of trading, which is nothing else but a trader's mindset. The term trading psychology refers to a specific state of mind that a trader usually has while he or she trades. If you don't have the right mindset, the odds will likely be turned against you.

Shape up Your Trader's Mindset

Traders can reshape their mindset by acting in a calm and relaxed manner. If you have correct knowledge of the subject and you have kept in place proper risk management guidelines, you need not be concerned about your trades at all. If a trade hits the stop-loss level, it doesn't mean that the world has ended for you. Traders lose trades all the time. It happens to even professional traders who have years of experience. Professional traders whose bread and butter rely on trading stocks have a winning rate of 50%. Even at this rate, you can bag sufficient profits on your capital if you trade with the right mindset.

You should practice the habit of not taking a losing trade to heart. There is nothing personal in a lost trade, although the temptation to make it personal runs high. The thought may start spinning in your head that you have lost something you could have easily won or you could have easily prevented. If you think like that, the need of the hour is to train your brain into thinking that markets tend to go upside and downside almost all the time. As a day trader, you should keep faith in the market analysis that you have already done. Just stick to the plan until the end of the day. Markets are void of emotions and if you start succumbing to your emotions, you will not be able to compete with the traders who don't let their emotions meddle in their trading transactions over the day. Try to nurture a morning routine for a more relaxed trading session. Try to wake up earlier, do some workout or a yoga session, and then sit on your desk with a heart full of faith in the homework you have done for the day.

Learn! Learn! Learn!

The education of the stock market is the key to success. It is one of the most important factors that play a key role in removing fear from your brain. This is what separates an average trader from a successful trader. Even if you have nurtured and developed the right mindset for trading, you cannot succeed until you have a solid knowledge base for the purpose. You must have a firm understanding of the reasons behind the price movements and market reaction. Similarly, I have hinted on how a market reacts to certain news and regular bonus reports. This will add more strength to your trader mindset. There are lots of concepts that are worth learning. However, you cannot learn them in a single session. You should make it a habit to internalize a concept daily so that your brain gets enough time to understand the slight nuances in the concept and to use the same during trading without having to open a book. You also can prepare and keep notes in a small diary for reference. You can form a healthy routine by consuming an hour before going to bed a good book on trading to clear out your basic concepts and bring them into practice during trading. You also can enroll in trading courses to boost your knowledge about stock markets.

The Mindset of a Successful Trader

Your psychology is going to be the major determining factor in bringing about the trading results that you are aiming at. Each trader keeps a unique belief system and it is their beliefs that determine how they trade and what results they get. The traders that have a weak belief system tend to fail even if they have the most profitable and seasoned trading strategy. What is a belief system? In simple words, it is called 'the trader's mindset.'

When you go through psychological issues, it is in your best interest to track the issues in your brain, recognize them, and then find a cure for them. Otherwise, you cannot fix them. A psychologist recognizes the issues and then tries to cure the patient. The process of curing a problem can take longer because the patients take long to recognize the problem and accept it as the source of their downfall. As a day trader, you need to take responsibility for your problems if you want to heal yourself. Success in trading is directly proportional to a sound and operational tracking system of your brain. It also is directly linked to a successful money management strategy, sound psychology, and proper capitalization during the day. These need to be in proper sync if you want to be successful in your trading ventures. Mastering your psychology is very well an ongoing process that goes on end until you are in control of your thoughts and decisions.

Ways to Acquire a Trader Mindset

The statistics are not quite positive for day traders as 80% of them are likely to lose money at one point or another. Usually, there is plenty of pressure on them for making money when you adopt trading as a full-time job. You pile up the pressure because you have to run your household with the money you earn from day trading. When you cannot do that and miss a day, you get under pressure that keeps mounting until you succeed in earning some money. But throughout the time you fail to earn, you are losing some. So, if you have lost $5,000 of your capital and have earned $2,500 back, you have failed. You have lost the entire $5,000 because the $2,500 you have earned back is likely to be spent on your daily expenditures. However, if you have a day job by which you can add up to your trading account quickly, you will face less pressure. Once the pressure of making money for daily expenditures is lifted from your nerves, you will be less inclined toward making emotional decisions. You will be able to maintain patience. There will be no quick profit-making or insane loss cutting. This is how you can be able to keep your head in the right condition.

Some traders get proper education on how to formulate a brilliant trading strategy and how to implement it, but they lose their calm along the way, which results in their losses. Day traders use a term called loss aversion, which means that losses can have a deep psychological impact on the brains of day traders. The impact is far greater than the positive effect that making gains in the stock market has.

Keep in check the emotions of greed when you are day trading. There comes a time when you are making lots of profit from the trade. You can do that once or twice, but you must not stick to it to make more. Once a stock has exhausted its run in the market, it can reverse any time and you will be left empty-handed, losing all the gains to the brutal reversal of the stock. The best strategy is to trace the signals and technical indicators and then stick to your strategy. When your calculations tell you to move out of your position, do that. Otherwise, you will see your trades turning against you, stripping you of early gains. This can be frustrating.

As a day trader, you need a plan for your day trading, such as which stock to choose and how to choose. Once you have made a plan and chosen a stock for trading, a trader mindset demands that you stick to the plan by exhibiting strict discipline. If you can do that, you will be able to kill emotional trading. You will have the satisfaction that you have a strategy that you must follow to stay in control of your trading positions. This will help you prevent shooting out of your trades over fears of reversal in trades.

Taking Profits, ROI and Passive Income

The primary objective for you to engage in day trading is to attain significant returns on your capital. For this aim to be attainable, you must apply productive strategies to your day trading involvement. In day trading, patterns in the stock price are bound to recur, and if you are keen, you can spot these trend repetitions. The recurrence may not match the actual price values, but the overall uptrends and downtrends may be identical. The time frame between the similar trends may vary between days and weeks, but the resemblance is noticeable when you sharpen your focus.

Based on these recurrences, you can take advantage of this knowledge to make profits from day trading. If you know how the stock price behaved last time, you can accurately predict its future movement. This assumption is valid as long as the circumstances and price patterns match. Using a price action chart, you can put your newfound strategy into action. A majority of these approaches involve looking out for an event called a breakout. The following scenarios describe various setups in which the breakouts favor entry into a particular trading position:

IPC Breakout

This breakout acronym stands for impulse, pullback, and consolidation. This phrase describes the behavior of the stock price on the price action chart. You need to look for a pattern characterized by these movements in the value of its stock. Usually, within the first few minutes, a cycle in Day Trading will start with a significant move in a specific direction in the form of an impulse wave. A pullback reaction typically follows this impulse wave.

A pullback is akin to applying instant brakes on the sharp initial impulse movement. From the pullback section, you will notice that the price hovers over a small range for a while. This period is the consolidation phase, where the stock price experiences a sideways movement. Note that the consolidation phase confines itself within the margins of the first impulse wave.

In the case of a fall in stock price beyond the open end, a different outcome may ensue. In this scenario, you will have both hovering and pullback happening at a value much lower than the opening stock price. At this point, your patience comes into play. You need to stand by for a potential breakout in the direction of the earlier impulse wave. Pay attention not to perform any trade in the event of a breakout in the reverse direction. The activation of a buying position is dependent on the stock price, breaking at a value that is greater than the consolidation level. For instance, in case the earlier scenario ensued and the stock price pulled back after an initial drop, trading is valid only when the breakout occurs over the consolidation.

When buying, it is advisable to take a long position on a small bid above the highest point of the consolidation phase. Taking a long trading position allows you to make a profit from a later increase in the price of the stock. In case you become interested in taking a short trading position, you can make an equally tiny bid below the lowest point of the consolidation.

A short trading position enables you to make a profit from a later drop in price. In both trading positions, you will determine your entry point based on a potentially favorable future outcome. This particular pattern setup is typical of the beginning of a trading session. Movements that take place close to the opening time are usually significant and potentially profitable. Always remember to discern the price action trends carefully before trading since any setup that lacks the distinctive sections is probably wrong.

RC Breakout

A reversal and consolidation breakout lacks the smaller pullback section found in, the earlier setup. In this case, you will have the usual significant impulse section followed by a much higher reversal. Note that the reversal occurs in a direction that is opposite to the impulse wave. The reversal section is immediate to the impulse without any signs of a preceding pullback. Due to the slight difference between RC and IPC breakouts, you need to pay special attention to the reversal trend. You should ignore any movement that occurs before the reversal. Wait for an imminent pullback from the reversal spike that ought to be smaller than your first or preceding impulse. The reversal wave now acts as your point of reference with which comparisons of the pullback and later consolidation take place.

Once you achieve a level of price consolidation, follow the guidelines as before in the earlier setup. If the breakout occurs either above or beneath the extreme points of consolidation, you can take a relevant trading position. Always bid small amounts of your capital in day trading since the margins are rather low, as well. An example of an RC setup involves an initial drop in the stock price of about 50 cents followed instantly by a reversal of, say 70 cents.

In this case, you need to concentrate your focus on the reversal rally of 70 cents that puts you back in the money anyway. The initial fall in price is the impulse wave, and it causes a distraction of which you should be wary. The more significant reversal should be your reference point, especially since you currently have an overall net trend of going upward. A pullback and consolidation phase should come after the reversal phase and finally accompanied by the awaited breakout.

Check for Reversal at Support and Resistance points

These two points signify the general pricing regions of a price action chart as opposed to real stock values. Support occurs when the falling trend of a particular stock price reaches its minimum point for that same trading cycle. The stock price cannot continue dropping beyond the support level. At support, the trend undergoes a period of consolidation before a reversal takes place. Upon reversing its direction, the price trend keeps rising to a point beyond which any further price increase becomes impossible.

This maximum level of the stock price is the resistance. Both support and resistance are typically indicative of how the various trading positions affect the movements of the stock market price. The economies of scale with the supply and demand forces are applicable here as well. In the context of day trading, excessive buyers lead to resistance, while support is the result of too many sellers. Once you identify the support and resistance regions, look out for the presence of consolidations at these levels.

A positive trading signal occurs in case of a breakout over the consolidation section at a support point. The same is valid for a breakout that happens beneath the consolidation at the resistance level. Beware of the market behaving unexpectedly. In rare circumstances, the stock price may breakout above the consolidation phase at the resistance level. In addition, the same might happen at the support region, and you encounter a breakout below the price consolidation. Although highly unlikely, these kinds of unusual breakouts are still possible. In such cases, you need to exit from your trading position immediately. You could use the breakout as your exit point. Therefore, your level of concentration has to be sharp to stay alert to such improbable eventualities.

Strong Area Breakout

This strategy enables you to participate in day trading above and below the resistance and support levels, respectively. These trending patterns are rare but still possible; hence, you need to develop and have a proper approach in place in case they arise. These regions located beyond the support and resistance points are the so-called strong areas. It is within these areas that you need to search for the relevant breakouts for you to conduct your trading.

First, you should take note of a trend that reached up to identical values at the resistance or support level multiple times. This pattern shows that the restrictive level is about to break. Based on the volume of trade in the stock market, such a trend is predictable. It is bound to break either its resistance or support. Trading on such values is often challenging because the margin beyond which the pattern exceeds the limit is usually small. You can decide to take a long position on a breakout trend that breaches the resistance.

However, beware of the lack of a sustaining rally beyond that level. Therefore, you should continue bidding only smaller amounts of capital on any breakout above the resistance level. The same reasoning applies to traders taking short positions on those breakouts that breach the support level. The amount of profit from such strong area breakouts is often insignificant compared to the larger margins experienced with the standard price action trading.

False Breakout

This type of breakout is useful as a confirmatory tool for other trading strategies. A false breakout is indicative of a price that attempts a particular movement, but fails and eventually goes in the opposite direction. For instance, consider an RC breakout setup where the reversal was higher than the initial impulse. After the reversal section, you would experience a brief pullback followed by a consolidation. Your expectation from the consolidation phase would likely be that the price takes an upward trend. This assumption is per the direction of the much higher reversal pattern.

However, due to the market forces, there is usually a small breakout downward for a brief moment straight after the consolidation phase. This breakout is false since the price would once again reverse and continue on its new upward trajectory. Knowing how to interpret and utilize false breakouts is essential in confirming the validity of your taken trading position. Using false breakouts in this manner is akin to proving a negative.

ROI

When you take part in day trading, you should expect a return on investment that corresponds to your input capital. Large amounts of capital outlay are typically disadvantageous due to the low rate of return. Investing in small amounts of money usually results in a more productive rate of returns. Success at day trading is often a prerequisite for you to attain a significant return on your investment. The following factors affect your capital's margins of profits directly:

Risk on Each Trade

This risk refers to the amount of your capital that is in danger of losing its value whenever you trade. It also refers to the trading position that you take every time you participate in day trading. For you to maximize your returns, you should have this risk under control. Risk management is achievable by setting a maximum limit on the amount of capital with which you can trade. For instance, you can set a limit of one percent of your available equity for commitment to a particular trade.

Also, use stop-loss orders to enforce this resolution. You need to adhere to these conditions strictly, every time you engage in any day trading transaction. It often becomes more comfortable to estimate your position size once you have both the stop-loss and entry point values. You need to realize that risk is a potential loss, and therefore, your aim must be to gain more money than you lose. You should learn to risk as little as possible while maintaining a higher margin for any probable profits.

Make Profits with Day Trading

Make Money with Day Trading

Before you start trading, look around the market and make your plan on which combination of currencies will you trade. This depends on the volatility of their exchange prices, which is based on research done on the past profitable exchanges. Planning also includes the time that you are willing to sit down and monitor the trades, make sure that you stick to the time scheduled to avoid messing up the already earned profit. Remember that choosing the time to trade should be at a time when the market is more active. The market will be there tomorrow and, therefore, when your scheduled time closes your trades. The strategy to be used throughout the time you are trading should also be thought out before you start trading, and it should be adhered to throughout the trading period in the day.

When day trading, you have to know how to manage your money because at the end of the day you want to have money, not lose money. During the day, you will take part in several trades, and therefore you need to know the amount of money you will use to invest. You have to prepare for losses and gains, but the total loss you expect is of importance to avoid losing all your money at the end of the day. This starts by knowing the risk per trade; this is the amount of money you are ready to lose on one trade. If you are a beginner, it is good to set your risk at a maximum of 2%. The size of the account should also be taken into account. If you have a trade that according to you, has a stop-loss of close to 50 pips, if you risk $200, your risk will be $4. This is done by dividing the amount of money you are risking by the stop loss pips.

Always have a stop target before you start trading, and also consider the type of market you are trading in; there are markets that are so dynamic such that your stop order might not be executed as per the set value. Therefore, to be safe, set your stops using the actual price-action and the conditions prevailing in the market, it is good to set them around the resistance, support levels, chart patterns, trend lines, and how volatile the currencies you are using are in the market. It is not only the stop loss position that you should consider during day trading, but also consider the point at which you want to take profits. For maximum profit, place appropriate levels of taking profit.

In addition, you should look at the reward-risk ratio, and when it is 1:1, it means that the amount you are risking equal to what you expect as a profit, and 3:1 has a triple amount to gain to lose. You can mix these such trades such that you have many with a high potential of gaining and few with an equal potential of winning. You can do it the other way around, but make sure that there is a balance that will leave you with some profit.

Although trading takes place at all times in the world, each market region has its own hours of trade. Therefore, as a trader, you should know your market and its opening and closing hours. You should also know that trading is not good throughout a trading day, and trading is good when the market activity is high. We have four major trading markets, and each of them has its own opening and closing hours. However, there are markets that open around the same time. For example, Tokyo market open at 7 P.M and close at 4 A.M while the Sydney market opens at 5 P.M until 2 A.M looking at the opening hours of the two markets, there is a time when they are all open, therefore, the level of activity with the currencies increases in the two markets between 5 P.M and 8 P.M when you are in the two markets, it is the best time to trade. This means that when more than one market is open at the same time, the trading activities are heightened, and the price of currencies fluctuates more. Therefore, maximize this by doing trades during the time when the market is very active.

You should also be alert on any news release that can make the price of the currency to fluctuate as you look out for changes in prices. Remember that the news can go against the predicted trend, and if you had already taken a position, you can either lose or gain, and it happens in seconds. You can make money by reacting correctly and within the correct time in day trading. The news to look out for is the GDP data, trade deficits, central bank meetings and announcements, consumer confidence, among other big news affecting the economy in the region.

As you look out for the fluctuations in prices, stay in check not to open so many trades that you cannot control. Having many trades does not mean that you will get a lot of money. The best thing to do is to start your trade in small portions. Identify three trades that show potential and monitor the trends; it is good to deal with two trades in a day that you will maximize on their profits than dealing with many that you will not make money on.

The amount of money made in the day also depends on the type of trading strategy used. To make more money choose a trading system that will give you more. When using scalping, it can help you to gain more, but you should increase the number of trades because the income obtained from one trade is very small. This is done when your main strategy is scalping. You can do more than one hundred trades in a day so that at the end of the day you have many wins than losses thus at the end of the day you have good money in your wallet.

If you are doing scalping as a supplementary strategy, you should use it when the market is not giving a large range in terms of the fluctuation of prices of currencies. In this case, most of the time, there are no trends in a longer time frame, and therefore using scalping in the short time frame becomes the best option to exploit. This way, you are assured that even without visible trends, there is a possibility that you will not end the day without money. This means that you initiate a long time frame trade, and as it develops, you start new sets of trade with a shorter time frame; it should be done in the same direction. You will then be entering and leaving the trade, as you collect small amounts, then later get a major profit with the long-time frame.

In a day, you can also use the false breakouts to make money in day trading. Looking at a trend, you can spot a breakout that you believe that it will not maintain the same direction. This is when you make a move, when the trend comes back to its original line; using this quick realization, you can make some cash. Using a fading breakout is the most effective because breakout tends to come out and out, and eventually, they succeed, with a fading breakout, you will be sure of making money. The rationale of using breakouts is that the resistance and support levels are known as ceilings and price floors respectively, and when one of them is broken, traders expect the trend to continue in that direction and therefore, the traders react in the opposite direction, which later stabilizes the trend to its original flow. An example is that when the resistance level is broken, most traders think that the price will continue in the upward trend and buy the currency instead of selling. You should, therefore, sell the currency, acting contrary to what everyone is doing, and when the breakout returns to normal, you buy again at a lower price. Similarly, when the support is broken, it means that the movement of the price is downwards, and most traders are likely to sell and not buy. To collect funds from this move, you should buy the currency instead of selling, and when the price resumes to its trend line, you sell it out. This type of trading is much profitable, but it can be very risky, therefore, analyze the graph well to make sure that it is a false breakdown before you enter the trade. However, to be safer, place a limit order when buying and selling, and make sure that at the end of the day, you have money in your wallet.

You can also make money using pivot points, which helps you to determine how prices of currencies are moving. Most of the time, the pivot points will identify prices as bullish or bearish, then represent the averages for the low, high prices, and closing prices occurring on a trading day. Do you need to know the market trend? The pivot points will help you with that. Use the pivot points to determine the general direction of the trade; if the market price of the currency is above the base of the pivot point, it suggests that the trade is bullish, and when it is below the pivot base, then it is bearish. In addition, when using pivot points, close all the long position trades when the market gets to the resistance levels and close the short ones when the market goes below the support level.

There is also the use of a reversal strategy that is commonly used around the globe; this strategy will help you to make money within a very short time, especially if the currency is moderately volatile. To use this strategy, you will have to study the graph to determine whether it has several consecutive highs and lows. At the highest point, which is called the top, you can easily predict that the price of the currency will reverse, and then react immediately by selling the currency. Similarly, if the graph of the currency has the lowest point, which is known as the bottoms, you predict that the trend will reverse, and buy the currency. When using this strategy, as long as you have predicted the reversal of the trend correctly, you will add money to your wallet.

Tips for Market Investing

Maximizing Your Investments

There are several ways that investors may maximize their investments. Of course, practicing proper trading techniques will help investors to earn greater returns on their investments. However, there are several other ways in which investors may maximize their investments and improve the returns on those investments. They may decrease investment costs, increase diversification, rebalance, and practice other techniques to improve their investments. It is important to learn about all the possible ways to maximize one's investments because you don't know what you don't know. Every bit counts. Just saving a bit here and there will quickly add up and maximize the investments.

Investors may maximize their investments by decreasing the cost of investing. There are several ways that investing may cost one money, and that money is coming directly out of the investment. Investors may switch from hiring a financial advisor to doing the investing themselves, cutting the costs of commission. Investors commonly forget about transaction costs. There is typically a flat fee for buying stocks through a broker. Instead of making many small purchases, investors may save up and only buy stocks in certain increments (for example, perhaps the investor won't buy more stocks until they have saved $1000). By doing this, a much smaller percentage of the investment is being cut out and used to cover those fees. This may require more patience, but that money will add up. Lowering one's expenses will increase their return. Instead of being spent, that money may be growing and earning a return on it. Because of compound interest, this money will earn money on itself and multiply over a period of years. This is why it's crucial to save every bit possible.

Investors must also really pay attention to their portfolios. Diversification is crucial, and it can save the investor from losing all of their investment. Markets typically fall much more quickly than markets rise. This means that the investor must prepare for such occurrences. It is important to regularly rebalance one's portfolio to ensure that it is positioned correctly for the investor to make the largest possible gains.

Investors must also truly pay attention to what they want. Maximizing one's investments will depend on the person and what their goals are. Although it is wise to listen to the advice of experts and see what other ways one may invest, it is crucial to follow the path that is best for the goals and preferences of the individual. This is why a plan is necessary and should be followed. Investors must not stop investing. This is another way to take advantage of compound interest. The investor's portfolio should never stop growing. This growth should be due to both growths in the investment and regular contributions by the investor themselves. Despite the great returns that may be experienced in a bull market, contributions are still necessary. Bear markets should also not discourage investors from continuing to invest; this can be a great time to get a good deal on a stock!

Retirement Plans

There are several savings plans that investors can get involved with. These can help to provide the investor with additional benefits that wouldn't be available to them otherwise.

One of these plans is a 401(k). This is a retirement savings plan that will be sponsored by an employer. This will allow the individual to invest their money before taxes so that they can save and invest some of their paychecks. The investor is not required to pay taxes until they withdraw this money from their account. Investors may control how to invest their money. It is common to have mutual funds that contain stocks, bonds, and money market investments. However, there are also target-date funds, which are stocks and bonds that will decrease in risk as the investor nears their retirement age. Unlike individual investing, however, this plan may not offer its users complete freedom. For instance, most employees must work for a company for a certain period of time before gaining access to their payments. Employees may even have to work for the company for a certain period of time before being able to enroll in a 401(k) at all. There are typical costs for withdrawing from these accounts before hitting retirement age as well. There are also contribution limits for each year. Investing for oneself, however, offers more freedom, and there are no limits on investing. For those working for an employer, however, this may be a good solution to investing using the paycheck given. It is a way to utilize the ability not to be taxed on one's investments from their paycheck. Employees may also enroll in Roth 401(k)s, which are not taxed for withdrawals. The better choice will depend on both the employee and the employer, as the plans are taxed differently.

403(b) plans are similar to 401(k)s, yet there are some slight differences. Both offer matching of the investments. For instance, for every dollar the employee contributes, the employer may contribute $0.50. This can prove to be greatly helpful to investors. The major difference between these are the employees that may enroll in these plans. Those in public schools, government jobs, nonprofits, and more may register for this plan. They are not for private-sector workers. Besides this, the plans are identical in their purposes. A 403(b) plan, however, may allow for faster vesting of funds and additional contributions, although the investment options may be less plentiful.

There are also IRA plans. These are plans to save for retirement. These plans have different contribution limits, tax rules, and penalties for early withdrawals. Traditional IRAs are plans that are set up to save for retirement by the individual instead of by a company. The owner of the account will make contributions to the account. To open an account, the individual must have earned income during the year and be under 70.5 years of age. Simple IRAs are set up by small business owners for their employees. Both the owner of the account and their employee will contribute. To open an account, the employee must follow any rules set by their employer. Roth IRAs do not give a tax break when contributing, yet the retirement withdrawals are typically tax-free. Those wishing to enroll in such a plan should research their options. If given the option, the individual should research the pros and cons of their options and decide which will provide them with the best way to reach their goals. Some may not have the option given to them, yet it is wise to educate oneself on where their money is going. This may help to allow the individual to see more ways to maximize their investments.

The Importance of Retirement Planning

The importance of retirement planning can never be overemphasized. This is because there is nothing important in life as having a well-prepared retirement plan. In the present day of elevated technology, we cannot be blamed for thinking of short-term goals like big-screen TVs, rather than getting ready for our futures. We are always coming up with excuses and explanations on why we delay these preparations and before we realize it, age catches up with us and it is suddenly too late to start planning.

Retirement planning, as we have already seen, starts with setting life goals that are clearly defined and assembling a financial plan that will enable you to achieve your goals after retirement. Planners must start planning early on so as to benefit from compound interest and also to steer clear of financial risk. The highest risk to a well-planned retirement is the possibility of living longer than your money.

Those who have had the misfortune of outliving their retirement funds have time and again found themselves living in absolute poverty or working until the day of their death. Others who depended wholly on the Social Security system have found it to be such disarray, and it is therefore wise not to depend entirely on this money. As a matter of fact, even Social Security is advising us not to count on it. According to financial experts, Social Security funds will only be able to cater for not more than 40% of the money the average person will need to live on upon retirement. That, to say the least, is a dreadful situation, but one that we will all have to live with, unless we start planning for the future in a sensible manner.

All in all, there is absolutely no reason why you must be caught unawares. The sooner you start planning, the sooner you will be able to relax, and the better it will be for you and those that you love. Seeing that you are bound to retire as one day, you must acknowledge the exact goals you wish to achieve in life.

On the other hand, if you have a spouse or next of kin, both of you should convene, exchange information and cooperate to make sure that what you are working at is what you both want eventually. The normal goals in life include creating families, studying hard so as to receive higher education degrees and setting money aside so as to leave your descendants well provided for, or to engage in charitable causes.

Direct Stock Purchase Plans

Direct stock purchase plans allow investors to directly purchase stock from the company without the use of a broker. These plans may be available directly to retail investors, yet some companies will use third-party administrators to handle the transactions. They will typically have lower fees and the potential for buying shares at a discounted price. This may not be an option for all companies. These plans may also come with restrictions on when the investor may purchase shares. This plan may appeal to long-term investors that lack the money for an initial investment otherwise.

The investor may choose to sign up once for this plan, or they may sign up to make automatic and periodic investments through a transfer agent. This agent will maintain balances and record transactions. To keep costs low, transfer agents will typically carry out bulk transactions for the company each time period that they choose. Direct stock purchase plans are an alternative to using online brokerages and they will typically cost less. Instead of paying higher transaction fees, the investor may pay a small purchase processing fee for each share that they purchase. These are usually quite a bit smaller than the transaction fees that investors must pay a brokerage. This means that the investor will have more money that they will be able to invest in. Instead of that money going to the brokerage, that money may be invested and generate a return for the investor. This can prove to be a wise move, especially for those wishing to buy a lesser amount of stocks. For those with greater funds for trading stocks, an online brokerage may prove more beneficial for the individual.

The Fear of Loss Is an Obstacle to Success

It has been established that people act very irrationally and even inadequately when they start losing money and this is very dangerous in a trader's job. The Bazerman phenomenon is very illustrative of such a situation.

Max Bazerman is a professor at Harvard Business School. Each year he sells to his students a 20$ banknote and always succeeds in collecting more than its face value. His record is the impressive amount of 204$. He shows the banknote to his students and tells them that he will give it to the one who pays the largest amount for it. But there is one tiny condition. The bidder who has remained second should also give to the professor the amount he was ready to pay before giving up.

Initially, the participants in the experiment expected that they had the chance for a perfect deal: pay less for something that is of greater value. Who would be such a fool to pay more than twenty dollars for a 20$ banknote? But the situation changes when the bid amount reaches the reasonable level and someone bids 19$. The one whose bid is slightly understanding that he is on the brink of losing and he will have to give money without getting anything. Therefore, he decides to raise the bet with 1$ in order to get the banknote. True, that is not a good deal any more, since the price is equal to the face value of the banknote, but at least he will not lose his money.

At this moment, the first one momentarily becomes second. Now he is in the position of the loser and faces the real and present danger of losing his 19$. This situation is so unacceptable that he would do anything to minimize his loss; therefore, he crosses the line of reason and bids 21$ for a banknote of 20$. It certainly looks silly to pay 21$ for a banknote of 20$, but the loss would be only 1$ and not 19$ as a while earlier.

From this point onwards, the bidding spiral may continue infinitely since both bidders have gone beyond the line of reason and the initially profitable deal has become absurd. In the end, both bidders have lost money, but one got the banknote and he actually lost 20$ less. The Bazerman phenomenon is a hands-on example of how:

Ambition for Profit Can Lead to Loss

Our inborn psychological intolerance to loss makes us push away the limit of loss that we are willing to accept; thus, retail traders very often suffer huge losses and even nullify their accounts. In other words, the fear of a minor loss can easily inflict huge financial damage. So the fear of losing is a major obstacle for beginners on their way to success. For many people, this ruins their further trading career.

Fear is an instinct in every living creature that helps them survive. In people, however, this instinct has also passed onto money, which stands very high up in the system of values of humans: as high up as life itself. This atavistic fear accompanies every beginner into the world of investment and trading on the financial markets.

Fear helps us avoid anything that we consider a threat. But we have to note that not all things that we consider threatening are really a threat. We just perceive it as such and until our mind is convinced that some kind of threat exists, our conscience perceives it as perfectly realistic.

That is why fear takes an active part in our trading decisions; therefore, it has a special place in this holistic trading concept. Just like ordinary people, those who are new to the trading career consider profit as the only acceptable choice, while loss makes them suffer beyond description. Bigger results lead to an outburst of euphoria, while accumulation of loss is a great psychological burden. We must acknowledge the fact that most of the mistakes committed by traders are due to fear. The major one is the fear of losing. But instead of protecting, this fear is an open door that lets in the greatest trouble for retail traders. There is even a paradox: the fear of suffering loss forces beginners into excessive risks in the hope that things will get better.

It is no secret to any trader that trading on the financial market is a risky business, and this undoubtedly means that there are certain risks in every deal. But we tend to disregard the risk which accompanies everything in life, thinking that by avoiding something unwanted, we make it less probable.

This way of thinking is wrong, but traders use it in trading. Being afraid of losses, they try to neglect risk and naively think that by not accepting loss, they increase their chances of a positive development in a given unfavorable situation. Therefore, one of the basic psychological trainings of a trader should be aimed at accepting risk and getting used to it.

Ultimately, there is nothing wrong with loss. It might be hard to believe, but loss and bankruptcy are very useful on the way to the highest levels in our profession.

The difference between a master and a beginner is that the master has failed more often than the beginner has tried.

But this understanding hardly fits into people's idea of life, where loss and especially bankruptcy are considered a failure. If a beginner has put all his money into his trading account, losing all this money might be the final blow to his trading career. Therefore, it is quite unreasonable to start trading with the total amount at one's disposal.

In this regard, I would strongly recommend beginners to start with a small amount and not the whole amount they could put aside for trading purposes. In this way, even if you lose a considerable amount, you shall not be kicked out of the game forever; it will only be an awakening. In this sense, bankruptcy could become a chance for a new beginning.

Vaccine for Creating Immunity

It is essential to realize that money lost in trading is not gone forever; with skills and discipline, we could always get it back and even earn much more. Fear in all its forms is one of the greatest obstacles on the way to success in trading. Many people think that fear keeps traders away from immature actions, while in reality, it is the other way around.

Actually, there is nothing fatal in trading on the financial markets, just financial loss. Besides, we could limit this loss to ranges acceptable to us. But fear expands the significance of this loss and in our mind, we perceive it as enormous.

Fear also urges us to start compensating the losses, and this reprograms our mind; it makes us impatient and more susceptible to mistakes. Thus, instead of moving away from the chart, patiently waiting for new favorable situations with a positive statistical expectation, we rush to restore the funds we lost.

In such situations, we are not capable of making good and reasonable decisions. Instead, we do the opposite; we act rashly and "bravely." We are inclined to ignore (temporarily) our own rules, and this immediately throws us into taking unacceptable risks. This is dangerous in any situation in our life, and in trading, it is a prerequisite for new and bigger losses.

Fear Makes Us Fearless

Fear is an instinct that keeps all living creatures away from danger, but in humans, it is in a subordinate position with regard to ego. Therefore, influenced by some dominating mobilization, our conscience ignores unfavorable information. In such a situation, we are not capable of taking correct and reasonable decisions; instead, we do the opposite, acting "bravely" and without thinking. We tend to ignore (temporarily) our own rules, taking unacceptable risks. This is dangerous in any situation in our lives, but when trading on the financial market, it is a prerequisite for new and more significant losses.

In their desire to avoid loss, beginners in trading increase the risk they have adopted initially. They move away from or entirely remove the waiting stop loss order when the price moves towards it on its way to activating it. In contrast to the well-considered initial stop at the opening of the deal, the mechanism of moving away always happens impulsively, fed by the hope that the price might change its direction at any moment.

There are, in fact, rare cases when the market is favorable, and in such cases, traders get away only with a lot of stress. But in most cases, there is also a considerable loss, which exceeds the reasonable level accepted by the beginner.

One's desire to turn out right is totally natural. It is not a pathological exception with trading beginners, due to man's inborn pursuit of perfection.

The human brain performs thousands of complicated functions. Based on this, our reason admits that we are faultless in our actions. Moreover, it strives to give us proof that we are right. Unwilling to admit mistakes, our mind refuses to accept information indicating that we are wrong. Instead, even when the market developments are against us, we concentrate only on what supports us, and when there is nothing positive, hope comes in place.

This way of thinking is very dangerous for every trader, but unfortunately, it is rooted in our mind. It turns out that when we have taken our decision to enter the market calmly and with argumentation, our judgment is much more correct than when taken later and pressed by fear. This happens even when we are winning.

A trader taken by fear is worried, even though the market is moving in his direction. His fear of losing makes him worry that the market might take back part of what he has gained or the whole of it. It is, in fact, not nice to lose part of the gains, and the thought of going back to zero could truly push you out of control.

Due to fear, when winning, the trader is inclined to ignore any information stating that the market has the potential to continue in his direction. Instead, he focuses only on the signals that his gains are in danger and usually exits the position much earlier than planned. This leads to the paradox that a trader caught by fear holds a losing position for a long time and then loses almost immediately after he starts gaining.

How to Think Like an Expert Trader

Know when to go off-book: While sticking to your plan, even when your emotions are telling you to ignore it, is the mark of a successful trader, this in no way means that you must blindly follow your plan 100 percent of the time. You will, without a doubt, find yourself in a situation from time to time where your plan is going to be rendered completely useless by something outside of your control. You need to be aware enough of your plan's weaknesses, as well as changing market conditions, to know when following your predetermined course of action is going to lead to failure instead of success. Knowing when the situation really is changing, versus when your emotions are trying to hold sway is something that will come with practice, but even being aware of the disparity is a huge step in the right direction.

Avoid trades that are out of the money: While there are a few strategies out there that make it a point of picking up options that are currently out of the money, you can rest assured that they are most certainly the exception, not the rule. Remember, the options market is not like the traditional stock market, which means that even if you are trading options based on underlying stocks buying low and selling high is just not a viable strategy. If a call has dropped out of the money, there is generally less than a 10 percent chance that it will return to acceptable levels before it expires which means that if you purchase these types of options what you are doing is little better than gambling, and you can find ways to gamble with odds in your favor of much higher than 10 percent.

Avoid hanging on too tightly to your starter strategy: That doesn't mean that it is the last strategy that you are ever going to need, however, far from it. Your core trading strategy is one that should always be constantly evolving as the circumstances surrounding your trading habits change and evolve as well. What's more, outside of your primary strategy, you are going to want to eventually create additional plans that are more specifically tailored to various market states or specific strategies that are only useful in a narrow band of situations. Remember, the more prepared you are prior to starting a day's worth of trading, the greater your overall profit level is likely to be, it is as simple as that.

Utilize the spread: If you are not entirely risk-averse, then when it comes to taking advantage of volatile trades, the best thing to do is utilize a spread as a way of both safeguarding your existing investments and, at the same time, making a profit. To utilize a long spread, you are going to want to generate a call and a put, both with the same underlying asset, expiration details, and share amounts but with two very different strike prices. The call will need to have a higher strike price and will mark the upper limit of your profits and the put will have a lower strike price that will mark the lower limit of your losses. When creating a spread, it is important that you purchase both halves at the same time as doing it in fits and spurts can add extraneous variables to the formula that are difficult to adjust for properly.

Never proceed without knowing the mood of the market: While using a personalized trading plan is always the right choice, having one doesn't change the fact that it is extremely important to consider the mood of the market before moving forward with the day's trades. First and foremost, it is important to keep in mind that the collective will of all of the traders who are currently participating in the market is just as much as a force as anything that is more concrete, including market news. In fact, even if companies release good news to various outlets and the news are not quite as good as everyone was anticipating it to be, then related prices can still decrease.

To get a good idea of what the current mood of the market is like, you are going to want to know the average daily numbers that are common for your market and be on the lookout for them to start dropping sharply. While a day or two of major fluctuation can be completely normal, anything longer than that is a sure sign that something is up. Additionally, you will always want to be aware of what the major players in your market are up to.

Never get started without a clear plan for entry and exit: While finding your first set of entry/exit points can be difficult without experience to guide you, it is extremely important that you have them locked down prior to starting trading, even if the stakes are relatively low. Unless you are extremely lucky, starting without a clear idea of the playing field is going to do little but lose your money. If you aren't sure about what limits you should set, start with a generalized pair of points and work to fine-tune it from there.

Something more important than setting entry and exit points, however, is using them, even when there is still the appearance of money on the table. One of the biggest hurdles that new options traders need to get over is the idea that you need to wring every last cent out of each and every successful trade. The fact of the matter is that, as long as you have a profitable trading plan, and then there will always be more profitable trades in the future which mean that instead of worrying about a small extra profit you should be more concerned with protecting the profit that the trade has already netted you. While you may occasionally make some extra profit ignoring this advice, odds are you will lose far more than you gain as profits peak unexpectedly and begin dropping again before you can effectively pull the trigger. If you are still having a hard time with this concept, consider this: options trading are a marathon, not a sprint, slow and steady will always win the race.

Never double down: When they are caught up in the heat of the moment, many new options traders will find themselves in a scenario where the best way to recoup a serious loss is to double down on the underlying stock in question at its newest, significantly lowered, price in an effort to make a profit under the assumption that things are going to turn around and then continue to do so to the point that everything is completely profitable once again. While it can be difficult to let an underlying stock that was once extremely profitable go, doubling down is rarely if ever going to be the correct decision.

If you find yourself in a spot where you don't know if the trade you are about to make is actually going to be a good choice, all you need to do is ask yourself if you would make the same one if you were going into the situation blind, the answer should tell you all you need to know.

If you find yourself in a moment where doubling down seems like the right choice, you are going to need to have the strength to talk yourself back down off of that investing ledge and to cut your losses as thoroughly as possible, given the current situation. The sooner you cut your losses and move on from the trade that ended poorly, the sooner you can start putting energy and investments into a trade that still has the potential to make you a profit.

Never take anything personally: It is human nature to build stories around, and therefore form relationships with all manner of inanimate objects, including individual stocks or currency pairs. This is why it is perfectly natural to feel a closer connection to particular trades, and possibly even consider throwing out your plan when one of them takes an unexpected dive. Thinking about and acting on are two very different things, however, which is why being aware of these tendencies is so important to avoid them at all costs.

This scenario happens just as frequently with trades moving in positive directions as it does negative, but the results are always going to be the same. Specifically, it can be extremely tempting to hang on to a given trade much longer than you might otherwise decide to simply because it is on a hot streak that shows no sign of stopping. In these instances, the better choice of action is to instead sell off half of your shares and then set a new target based on the updated information to ensure you are in a position to have your cake and eat it too.

Not taking your choice of broker seriously: With so many things to consider, it is easy to understand why many new option traders simply settle on the first broker that they find and go about their business from there. The fact of the matter is, however, that the broker you choose is going to be a huge part of your overall trading experience, which means that the importance of choosing the right one should not be discounted if you are hoping for the best experience possible. This means that the first thing that you are going to want to do is to dig past the friendly exterior of their website and get to the meat and potatoes of what it is they truly offer. Remember, creating an eye-catching website is easy, filling it will legitimate information when you have ill intent is much more difficult.

First things first, this means looking into their history of customer service as a way of not only ensuring that they treat their customers in the right way, but also of checking to see that quality of service is where it needs to be as well. Remember, when you make a trade every second count, which means that if you need to contact your broker for help with a trade, you need to know that you are going to be speaking with a person who can solve your problem as quickly as possible. The best way to ensure the customer service is up to snuff is to give them a call and see how long it takes for them to get back to you. If you wait more than a single business day, take your business elsewhere as if they are this disinterested in a new client, consider what the service is going to be like when they already have you right where they want you.

With that out the way, the next thing you will need to consider is the fees that the broker is going to charge in exchange for their services. There is very little regulation when it comes to these fees, which means it is definitely going to pay to shop around. In addition to fees, it is important to consider any account minimums that are required as well as any fees having to do with withdrawing funds from the account.

Pitfalls to Avoid

Knowing the best practices is not enough to succeed in the stock market. You also need to know the pitfalls that you will encounter along the way. It is important that you take note of these pitfalls and blunders to avoid committing the same mistakes. It is worth noting, however, that many of the pitfalls are quite hard to avoid, especially for a beginner. So, do not beat yourself too hard if you still commit them. But, be sure to learn from every mistake that you make and try to do better next time. Many of the world's greatest stock traders have experienced many pitfalls in their careers. The important thing is for you to continue to learn and grow as a stock trader. Experiencing some pitfalls is a normal part of development. But, of course, try to avoid them as much as possible.

Chasing After Your Losses

This is a pitfall that is simply difficult to avoid. In fact, even those who are aware of the consequences of chasing after one's losses still commit this mistake. The temptation is just too strong to ignore. But it is important that when you encounter this pitfall, you need to control yourself. A good way to prevent this from happening is by having a better understanding of how it works. Chasing after one's losses usually happen right after a bad loss. The thing is that many traders expect to suffer some losses; however, once an important trade fails, which causes a strong negative impact on their funds, then they feel and think that the only way to recover from their loss is by chasing after it. Keep in mind that in stocks, your profit will be a percentage of your investment, for example, 10%, 50%, 80%, or even 250%, etc. Hence, the higher that you invest in a trade and if it gives a positive outcome, you will earn more money provided that you invested a higher amount. This is exactly how people chase after their losses. In a way, it is logical, which makes it appear like a convincing move. After all, once you lose 30% of your total investment, you will have to make lots of correct investments just to recover the said loss. If you want to recover more quickly, then you can invest the remaining 70% in once trade.

The problem here is that chasing after your losses is not good for your bankroll. This is because when you chase after a loss, you will have to invest a higher amount—usually, an amount that is no longer fit for your strategy. It can suddenly turn your approach into an aggressive one, and your bankroll will most probably not be able to handle it for a long-term. For example, instead of just investing 2% per trade, an aggressive strategy may compel you to suddenly invest 25% of your investment per trade.

Although there is still a chance that chasing after your loss may end up with a positive outcome, it is still not recommended, because it entails higher risks which you can otherwise minimize.

So, what should you do? Well, just before you invest in any stock, make it clear in your mind that you may lose your whole investment and that every trade that you enter into may not end with a positive outcome on your part. Be open to the idea of losing your investment. Also, have a plan ready on what you will do in case that you lose a series of trades consecutively. In other words, prepare for the worst. Also, instead of focusing on chasing after your losses, a better approach for you is to accept all the losing trades that you encounter and focus on developing your strategy. After all, the only way to recover your losses is to make more profit, then you need to work on your trading strategy.

It is also worth noting that investing more money in a trade does not always mean that you will profit more. The only assurance is that you are risking a bigger amount of money. The important thing is still to be able to identify profitable stocks to invest in. For example, let us say that person A invests $50,000 all at once, while person X only invests $1,000 in different stocks. If the investment of person A turns out to be a bad investment, then he will suffer a corresponding percentage of his invested amount, a loss. However, if person X's investment turns out to be a good investment, then he will profit. Indeed, it may be just a small amount, but it is still a profit nonetheless. Instead of chasing after your losses, you need to focus on increasing your rate of success. Strive to come up with a reliable strategy that will allow you to trade many times with a high success rate.

Not Testing Your Trading Strategy

A normal part of the life of any stock trader is to continuously develop his strategy. Take note that the stock market continues to develop just as businesses and consumers continue to evolve. If you want to have continued success in the stock market, then you have to work on your strategy on a regular basis. There is also no one best strategy for all occasions. There are so many circumstances that can affect the prices of stocks in the market, and you should be flexible enough to make adjustments in your strategy. But how do you know if your strategy is already good enough? Well, you need to test it in a real market situation. This is where you may find a demo account handy. Or, if you want, you can just run your own simulation without placing any real trade. You can also just trade a very small amount. The important thing is that you test your strategy before you use it with a considerable amount of money.

Another important thing to be noted is that you can expect to change your strategy from time to time. Again, you should be flexible enough to deal with changes. It can be changes in the economy, consumer behavior, competition, and the latest trends, among others. Now, every time that you make any changes in your strategy be sure to test it several times. Even a small change in strategy can have a significant impact, so it is important that you test your strategy, as well as any modifications that you make.

Using the Same Losing Strategy

It is also not uncommon to find people who continue using the same strategic thinking that since the strategy has already lost several times, then it is already due to make a good hit. This is a completely erroneous understanding. It is worth noting that the stock market does not have a mind of its own. It does not remember or care whether you lose or win many times in a row. Keep in mind that every trade that you make is independent of all other trades. Every trade is also not connected to any past trades that you have done. Hence, just because you already lost five times in a row does not mean that the next trade that you enter into will be a profitable one. Therefore, it is important that every trade that you make should be back up with sufficient research and analysis.

It is worth noting that even the best strategies out there also fail to make a profit from time to time. There are simply so many things that can happen in an investment, considering that there are many factors that affect the stock market. Hence, you cannot expect your strategy to win 100% of the time. However, when a strategy has already lost several times, and it appears that it generates more losses than profits, then you should examine the strategy and decide if you still want to use it. Sometimes a strategy just needs a little bit of adjustment; however, sometimes it would be better if you completely abandon a strategy if it is not effective enough.

Pump and Dump

The pump and dump is a common scheme in stocks. It is worth noting that even though most traders are aware of this fraudulent scheme, there are still many who fall for it. So, how does it work?

In a pump and dump scheme, a person promotes his stocks, usually with the use of some marketing hype. Considering today's age where you can easily spread a word to the world with just a click of a mouse, it is now easier to execute this scheme. Of course, the promotion will highlight the stocks being promoted to make it look like a nice investment. Due to the increased attention and interest that the promotion will generate, the price of the promoted stocks will tend to increase. This, of course, will look as if it is a good choice for an investment. As a result, it will look more attractive to investors, which will cause some investors to buy the promoted stocks. Now, this is where the problem will kick in. The moment the stocks are sold at a higher price than its actual value, the promotion will cease and the true value of the stocks will be revealed. Since the value of the stocks only increased due to the promotional hype and not because of legitimate factors, the price of the stocks will now begin to fall. As you can see, the outcome is that the one who exercised the pump and dump scheme gets a nice profit while the buyers pay and get in possession of losing stocks.

When people buy stocks, they usually favor stocks that are being promoted. Although this is a good thing, you should be careful about it. Be sure that it is not a pump and dump scheme that you are buying into. The sad truth is that even some so-called "experts" take advantage of their name and also commit this scheme for their own gain. This is another reason why you should develop your own understanding of the stock market and not merely rely on "experts," for many of these "experts" are not real experts but merely promote themselves to be like so.

The pump and dump is not always a bad thing. In fact, if you take a closer look at the process, you can use it to work on your advantage. As you can see, there is a part of the process where the price of the promoted stocks increases. This is an opportunity to profit. The key here is to be able to identify a pump and dump scheme just before it begins or immediately in its early stage so that you can take advantage of it. By purchasing some of the promoted stocks, you can enjoy the effects of the promotion. However, you need to be sure to sell the stocks just before their price begins to drop. So, do not be too greedy. To be safe, decide to make a sell order even while the promotion is still ongoing.

It is also worth noting that just because there are stocks that are being promoted does not always mean that their value will increase. The effectiveness of the promotional campaign must also be considered.

Develop a Trading Plan

Even if you find a risk-reward ratio that suits your appetite (or tolerance) for risk—this doesn't mean that you are achieving it. Use your trade log to evaluate your results and compare that to your target risk-reward. It's perfectly fine to adjust your risk-reward number; calculating it allows you to adjust to realistic numbers sometimes.

If you are on limited funds, don't rush it and dig yourself a hole that is difficult to get out of. If you lose a percentage of your account, here's

If you lose this % PERCENTAGE	You have to make this to get back to even PERCENTAGE
5%	5.26%
10%	11.11%
15%	17.65%
20%	25.00%
25%	33.33%
30%	42.86%
35%	53.85%
40%	66.67%
45%	81.82%
50%	100.00%
$y = x/(1-x)$ where X=lost %	

what it takes to make it up.

Win Rate versus Reward-Risk Ratio Computations

Example: See "25%" in the table below, reward: risk = 3:1 target $60 and risk $20, or target $75 and risk $25, still 3:1 you must win 25% of trades with target profit to break even (B/E).

In your trade log, be sure and include notes on each trade's results in terms of reward: risk. Find out your trading stats and then refer to this table to see what adjustments or improvements you need to make.

This is likely the most valuable table of all. You might want to copy it and put in up in a prominent place at your trading station. Getting this combination right is key to successful trading. There are times when you must adapt to survive, no matter how much experience you have. Do not assume so quickly that you can use one ratio to trade all four micros.

Win Rate for B/E	Reward	Risk	Risk Reward Ratio
66.7%	1	2	0.5
50.0%	1	1	1

33.3%	2	1	2
28.6%	2.5	1	2.5
25.0%	$60.00	$20.00	3
22.2%	3.5	1	3.5
20.0%	4	1	4
18.2%	4.5	1	4.5
16.7%	5	1	5
15.4%	5.5	1	5.5
14.3%	6	1	6
13.3%	6.5	1	6.5
12.5%	7	1	7
11.8%	7.5	1	7.5
11.1%	8	1	8

10.5%	8.5	1	8.5
10.0%	9	1	9
9.5%	9.5	1	9.5
9.1%	10	1	10

Suggestions for Improvements

For you to win as a trader, you don't have to have an extremely high win-rate—or a large reward-to-risk ratio. As long as your reward-to-risk ratio and your historical win-rate match, you can expect some positive results.

By keeping an accurate trading log, you'll have the numbers you need to help you move towards your goals. It might be that you change your ratio, or you establish a new average win-rate by changing your strategies, such as entry-rule or exit-rule.

Keep an Accurate Trade Log, Then

1. See what your average winning amount is.

2. Then compute your average losing amount is.

3. See what your ratio win rate is (percentage of winners).

4. While doing this, you need to evaluate if:

   a) You take profits too quickly

   b) If you are allowing losers to get too large before you exit

Other Adjustments You Can Make

See what you might change to improve. (Example: Are you trading too often, or not enough? Should you reconsider your trade entry criteria? Should you reconsider your trade exit criteria?

Do you get better results during certain trading hours? Can you change trade times to make an improvement?

How many of your trades, if any, are going against a strong trend. Remember: going with the trend makes trades less risky. Trading with the day's trend is less risky.

Are you reviewing the day's major reports due out?

Have you reviewed the day's news, so you are aware of any important times and events on the current trading day?

Self-Evaluation

- What are the things you do best? Worst?
- Do you maintain control of your emotions when trading?
- Is there any way you can adapt during a trade to improve your trading?
- Do you do just as well when you trade 2 hours a day as you do when you trade 4 hours?
- Are you using the correct types of orders? You should rarely use market orders, use limit orders instead.
- When you identify a weakness, what can you study to improve and/or get some new ideas? What resources can you use to find solutions?
- What emotions visit you when you realize you missed a good trade, due to a lapse of attention?

Remember, you can learn from hindsight, but don't judge yourself by it. The perfection in hindsight is just an illusion, nothing more. It is a false target, trying to replicate it is futile, a total waste of time.

If you practice by always trying to catch the "carrot on a stick" (an impossible goal), that is what you will learn. Do not practice the impossible, practice for the results you need. You not only need to win; you need to learn money-management (aka how to lose without accumulating large losses).

Another common mistake for beginners is to switch trading methods too quickly and too often. You need to give your method time for you to learn how to use it. When you try five different methods in a day and you are constantly changing—you may not be allowing yourself enough time to learn it. Doing this will drastically slow your progress.

Be sure to note in your trade log, the hours you are trading. As a business person, you need to evaluate your pay per hour, per day, or per week... Just like any other job.

I know many traders that only trade one to two hours per day. If you can learn to do your very best for 90 minutes a day and make money, you might do better scaling up your trades instead of simply "trading more hours."

I have a friend, a very successful trader who trades 90-minutes a day, no more and no less. He told me that he has learned that he is more successful making fewer trades, and on many days, he places no trades at all. A forced trade when you are bored, or you feel are obligated to trade every day—can be a poor trading habit. My friend told me that his attitude is that if the market doesn't provide him a good opportunity, he just doesn't do any trades that day. Most traders don't have that much discipline. It sounds easy to just "wait for a good trade," but it's actually something a lot of traders just never learn to do.

Sometimes just changing your rules until you trade fewer trades can make a huge difference in your win-rate.

Here's an example of writing down a trading plan, a vital part of developing your own trading strategy. It's a good idea to keep a dedicated ledger or notebook of your trading plan and its evolution. This can be a valuable way to track your progress.

Forming Your Trading Plan

Reward-risk ratio: 3 to 4 to one

Reward-risk amounts: $60-$80 versus $20-$25 loss

Entry rules:

a) Trade with the prevailing trend

b) Use resistance/support and MACD signals

c) Trade one contract for now

d) Identify the stop loss point level

e) Identify entry point level

f) Identify point ranges during 5, 10, 15-minute intervals to help determine reward-risk amounts

g) Have an exit plan

h) Do not trade against the trend (it's riskier)

Exit rules: Use a stop-loss order to fix losses, then try for an exit near target or greater.

Of course, this example is very basic, but it is a starting place—and sometimes, just a simple basic plan can work much better than a complicated one.

Trading is your business, your side-hustle. The trade plan is your logistics center. The trade log is the accounting department that gives you the bottom line on how your company is doing. Your internet connection, computer, pad, or phone, and your broker's software are your physical plant. Fortunately, most of your physical plant is a one-time expense and won't need many upgrades. Since you probably already had your phone, computer, and internet—your startup cost (investment) is limited to the investment capital you start with—and of course, your time invested.

Don't forget to critique yourself in the "big picture" frame of reference. For example, you might be winning 50% of your trades and still be experiencing a net loss. 50% is a high win-rate, but your reward-risk ratio could be costing you money. This could mean you are letting losses run past your limits or taking your profits too soon. Or maybe you need to look at adjusting something as simple as your entry rules, how many trades you do, or how many days per week you trade. Forget about imitating other traders, you need to find what works for you.

Advice to Beginner's on Day Trading

Day trading is not simple at first. Skills have to be built and some policies are set. All in all, it is a learning process that calls for patience and perseverance. Let us look at various fields at how you can get motivated this good day.

Day Trading Strategies for Beginners

- **Financial analysis**: Well, money is a very important asset. With that in mind, you need to be super careful in how you plan on using it. Failing to plan is planning to fail. Beginners are advised to use just a little amount of capital for a start-up until the time they are fully experienced in the day trading track. Most of the traders do not have more than 2% of the capital in the trade. Furthermore, as a beginner, always consider slow but sure steps. Get to grow little by little. This is a journey with lots and lots of protocols to learn and master with a successful and rich endpoint.

- **Seek every kind of learning material**: Learning makes you educated on what you are actually doing. It makes you informed, you get to learn every living trick in that particular field (day trading). Take each day as a learning day in that you get to learn something new in a particular section. You get to grow. Being involved in day trading is a course journey itself. Below are some sources of learning materials for day trading:

- **Videos**: Videos provide practical learning sources and that is why they end being so famous. Explore several video learning contents from sites like YouTube.

- **Articles, blogs, etc**: Day traders from different places of the world like to engage their experiences from the moment they started trading. As a beginner, seek the beginner level kind of sources. Read their experiences widely, take down important facts, and ask questions—recommendations. With that, even the confidence and the thrust force to begin day trading will highly be enlightened.

- **Trends**: Get to follow each and every trend and get the idea of what is actually happening. They are highly educative when it comes to future prediction analysis.

- **Consistency or stability**: Another idea to add, day trading is quite logical. Day trading cannot be analyzed by fear or even greed. Mathematical approaches have to be considered. Set strategies have to be put in place too! Examine every logical operation bound to happen during day trading so as to possess certain clear stability. Once stability has been established, expect some big-time profit rates and an excellent reputation.

- **Timing**: The trading market becomes volatile every single trading day. Experienced traders have mastered the moves and so they are quite sure about what steps to take next once they get to read the structures. For beginners? Quite not sure of what move to take. A slow but sure protocol is fundamental too. As a beginner, do not be quite in a rush to predict. Take one or more time to examine every single trend and get your desired prediction. Do not be too slow though, you may end missing so much.

- **Scalping**: the scalping kind of strategy takes advantage of the small kind of prices that happen drastically during the day trading sessions. This kind of mechanism involves getting engaged so quickly and so fast and then leaving right away.

How to Reduce Losses when Day Trading

Day trading is made up of both losses and wins. The odds of both occurrences happening during trading are so high. We do try our best to win, and in the end, we do win frequently, but in the end, losses never miss too. Below are some the ways in which we can reduce losses in our day to day training activities:

Manage Your Risk

Managing your risk at an individual trade is so important. It is super advisable that on a single trade you should not risk above 1% of your balance in the account. Taking an account setup of $100,000 then a trader should not stake more than $1,000 on single market trade. With this information principled out, there are zero chances that one-point loss risks the loss of everything.

Consider Using Limit Orders

The use of limit orders is applicable for buying and selling. While the sell limit order will be used to sell stocks once it is above or equal to limit price, buy limit order will purchase it when it is below.

Bottom Line

Traders should always understand when they have intentions to enter and/or exit a trade before execution. By applying stop losses cautiously, a trader usually minimizes huge losses while avoiding the number of counts a trade is usually dumbed needlessly.

Setting up Stop-Losses and Take-Profit Points

A stop-loss is a point at which a trader has preset as a mechanism to stop his/her losses by disposing the trade at a loss whereas take-profit point being inverse is the actual price point at which a trader will cash in on the trade taking the profit already acquired on the margin difference. A stop-loss occurs when a trader had experiences that had not been planned. The points are designed to curb the "give it a little time" mentality of trading while limiting the unintended losses before they rise higher. On the other hand, take-profits occurs when the additional upside is limited given some risks.

Establish a Daily Stopping Point

As you set up some general strategies, decide on how much you are willing to risk per everyday trading session. Remember, if you make the choice to set your stopping point based on average trading performance, the amount of time you are expected to lose is higher over a span of period as you continue to learn and master new styles during everyday trading sessions.

Take a Wide Look at Your Expected Return

Implement the formula in several day trading occurrences and compare the output and get to select the ones with the highest profit expectation rates.

Put Options

Put options give you the chance to sell an underlying stock at a specified price during or at the blink of the expiration of a given option.

Planning Your Trades

Plan the trade and trade the plan. So as to secure yourself as the winner in a certain war, it will cost you to prepare for that. Preparing basically means setting up some strategies, really good strategies that will clearly thrust you forward and generally excel at the end game. Outline realistic strategies and at the end plan for your trades.

Conclusion

A couple of reminder tips to help keep your capital safe when it comes to the time to hit that button and set your first trades into motion.

- Always, always, always include a stop-loss order in your trade. This is one of the basic components of a trade and the most important because it protects you from excess risk. For a short position, place it above the market. For a long position, place it below. That way, if the market does not follow your desires, you are protected.

- Do not ever move that stop-loss order in the opposite direction to your position. You can move it in the same direction, by all means, if you want to increase your profits, but to move it in the opposite direction you are caving to fear.

- Use the same information you used to help you open a position to decide when it's time to close that position. For example, keep an eye on what the volume price analysis is saying about the market's movement, use the currency matrix to decide whether the currencies you are trading in are strong or weak, use the currency strength indicator to look for trends and keep an eye on the news to see what major developments are happening.

There is no right or wrong answer when you're deciding how to make the market work for you—perhaps you'll be happy as a short-term trader, maybe you prefer to be long-term; perhaps you prefer one style of analysis to another and find that you make better decisions when you rely on a specific combination.

The only golden rule is to remember your risk levels and always stick to them, come what may. Maintain that capital and it will always be there to work for you, earning you those small but consistent profits that, over time, can build into an incredible nest egg.

Practice makes perfect, so go ahead and experiment as you dip your toes in the water. If you have capital to spare, feel free to experiment with real money and real trades. If you prefer to be more cautious, there is absolutely nothing wrong with the idea of "pretend trades" before you risk your real savings.

The upcoming step is going to be to stop reading and to start preparing yourself to trade in the forex market successfully. When you are getting ready to get started, you are going to want to do what you can to ensure that you keep your emotions in check at all times while also doing what you can to keep your expectations in check in terms of your early success rates. Additionally, it is important to consider the fact that the most reliable profits will come not from risky choices but from dedicated research and excellent timing.

It cannot be stressed enough that the secret to success in this business relies on your own determination and drive. It is those qualities that will motivate you to dig deep into the social and economic challenges that propel this market to find that one gem, that one kernel that could yield you untold rewards. It can be a wild and exciting ride if you have the wherewithal to stand it. There are lots to be gained if you do.

Make sure you test your strategies out and put them into practice while they are still fresh in your mind. But I am sure that if you do, you will find yourself well on your way to exciting and life-changing profits that await you in the future.

Many people are turning to trade in order to generate their income, invest in their future, or simply give themselves extra cash for the month. Whatever your reason is for getting into trading, you learned four different types of trading strategies within the contents of this. First, you learned position trading, which allows you to hold your position for months to a year. Second, you learned about swing trading, which focuses on the position you hold for a few days to a couple of weeks. Third, you were given some information on day trading, which focuses on buying and selling all your trades in one day and finally learned about scalping trading, which is often called the minute strategy as you hold a position only for a few seconds to a minute or two.

Now you not only understand these four strategies better, but you also understand the basics of forex trading. You also understand the basic risks involved, have the know-how needed to achieve the winning